Flavorful Shortcuts to Indian/Pakistani Cooking

Cover Photo:
Farhana, teaching a cooking class at
The International Culinary Arts School at The Arts Institute of Los Angeles,
in Santa Monica, California

Flavorful Shortcuts to Indian / (Pakistani) Cooking

Simplified Tandoori Cooking Curried Dishes Vegetable Dishes Desserts and more...

Farhana Sahibzada

PHOTOGRAPHS BY
Dr. Afzal Sahibzada

www.flavorfulshortcuts.com

Order this book online at www.trafford.com
or email orders@trafford.com

Most Trafford titles are also available at major online book retailers.

Printed in the United States of America.

ISBN: 978-1-4120-3714-3 (sc)
ISBN: 978-1-4669-4138-0 (e)

Library of Congress Control Number: 2012910408

Trafford rev. 04/22/2014

 www.trafford.com

North America & international
toll-free: 1 888 232 4444 (USA & Canada)
fax: 812 355 4082

To maintain an *'exotic feel'* in print, the English in this book has an Indian flavor designed carefully to match my south Asian accent.

"Designed to **_inspire_** not _impress_ the reader"
A book that shares it all, with no family secrets held back.

Quick and easy versions of some popular Indian/Pakistani recipes
stemming from cooking classes conducted by
Chef Farhana Sahibzada
in Southern California and Internationally over a twenty year period

Flavorful Shortcuts to Indian/Pakistani Cooking

For

Mehnaz, Naureen and Omar

and

All the young chefs in the family.

CONTENTS

VEGETABLE DISHES THE INDIAN/PAKISTANI WAY

LENTILS

CHICKEN CURRY DISHES

FLAT BREADS AND NAANS

Conducting a Cooking Class
in Westlake Village, California

At a cooking class in Santa
Monica, California

INDIAN/PAKISTANI DESSERTS

HOT AND COLD BEVERAGES

An
Early Morning
Trip to The
Farmer's Market!

Fresh from the farm, luscious ripe tomatoes!

Potatoes, abundant in variety and shades

Some Flowers for the Dinner Table as Well . . .

Fresh Ingredients Ensure a Flavorful Meal!

Shopping at the local 'farmer's market' for the best of produce! Starting with the best Ingredients is the key to a fine end result!

Special Thanks

Munkee AKA Buggy Boy
The good Guy . . .

Gugu AKA "Ghunda"*
(* 'The Rascal")
Do not let these 'innocent'
looks fool anyone

To my cats, Munkee and Gugu for keeping me company during my work
on this project
They worked hard for me

ACKNOWLEDGEMENTS

This project took its final shape with direct and indirect support of many well wishers and influencers, some of whom may not even be aware of how meaningful their feedback and assistance has been. I owe gratitude to each and everyone for their backing, support, involvement and most of all encouragement.

Starting from my husband, who has been a constant source of appreciation and encouragement for my cooking from the time when I was barely learning how to boil rice.

I would also like to thank my daughters Mehnaz and Naureen for their constant love, encouragement, wide eyed excitement and loud cheers for my every little accomplishment.

I owe thanks also to all my nephews and nieces for hailing me as a star in the kitchen during my visits to Lahore, Pakistan and being my sous-chefs as we all cooked, shared laughter and created memories together.

My thanks also to all the friends, family and professionals who have been generous in sharing their special techniques and showing me the step by steps of their prized recipes.

I would like to thank all the cooking schools in California that believed and continue to believe in me and my work and offer me opportunities to help grow my career especially:
Ms. Marian Suckut at Pierce College Extension in Woodland Hills, Chef Christophe Bernard and his wonderful faculty at Culinary Arts Institute in Santa Monica, Ms. Phyllis Vaccarelli at Let's Get Cookin' in Westlake Village and Ms. Jennifer Haigh and Sunshine at Whole Foods Markets, Tarzana. Thanks also to Ms. Barbara Spector, Mr. Sajid Ali Baig, Royal Delhi Palace in Canoga Park,

California and India Sweets and Spices in Canoga Park, California for their continued help with my cooking classes.

Very special thanks to Mehnaz, Amy Rocha and Dr. Seemie Zoberi for their advice and valuable feedback of my work.

Many thanks to Ms. Jacquelyn Kinkade Silberberg and Dr. Iris Shah for their painstaking, generous and selfless effort of editing and proofreading my work.

I am especially grateful to Ms. Joanne Weir, the award winning food writer, cooking teacher and TV personality for her time and the precious gift of writing the foreword for my book.

To Mehnaz, Natalie and Mike Clarke for being test chefs for my recipes and to Naureen for having the sincere intent of being one. (This is a mother/daughter joke, she will get around to it in between her patients, I know it)

I would also like to extend a very special thank you to Mr. Dana Martin and all my friends at ITT Technical Institute in Sylmar, California for giving me the opportunity to turn their lunch room into my *test kitchen*; and for their encouraging critique and feedback of my recipes.

And most of all, a very special thank you to my mentor and life-coach Ms. Eve Ray whose priceless support and guidance inspires me in more ways than she can imagine.

And finally, I am thankful for a warm upbringing in a creative home and for parents that passed on to us a love of good food, blooming flowers and hearty laughter.

FOREWORD

My mother taught me a lot of things but one of the things I remember most is what she always said, "You have to eat every single day three times and why not make it special?" I grew up with the philosophy that cooking is a part of life and sitting down to enjoy it with family is an essential part of everyday.

That's easy to say, but not always easy to do. We're all going a thousand miles an hour. I'm no exception! This year alone, I launched a direct-to-consumer wine label, -Joanne Weir Wines, opened my first restaurant, Copita in Sausalito, CA, created an iPad app, and executive produced my new PBS cooking show, Joanne Weir's Cooking Confidence. That's on top of my usual cooking classes, culinary tours in the Mediterranean and writing magazine articles.

But I'm not the only one living a full-plate life. I bet you're doing the same and somehow cooking good food at home has been placed on the back burner.

Yes, lack of time is an excuse but there's also a confidence issue . . .

Last year, when I was trying to decide what to call my new television series and companion cookbook, I took a survey asking everyone I knew what were their obstacles in the kitchen. Again and again I heard the same answer . . . Lack of confidence. I was so surprised. Just because I came from a long lineage of professional cooks, my Mom, grandfather and great grandmother, I thought everyone had confidence in the kitchen.

Whether it's a working single mom struggling to get a decent dinner on the table, a fireman learning to whip eggs whites for a soufflé he's been longing to learn how to make, or a 12-year old smiling like a Cheshire cat as she makes her first chocolate fudge cake on my TV program, I never get tired of getting people excited about food and teaching them to cook. There's something about that wonderful "ah-ha" moment when someone says "I made this—and it's delicious! I can do it."

When anyone steps into the kitchen, gives cooking a shot and are successful at mastering a recipe, that experience gives them the confidence to try another. Then the next time, the thought of cooking something new and different doesn't seem so daunting. Once the confidence factor is licked, then cooking and eating good food at home is a reality.

This is where Farhana's book, —*Flavorful Short-cuts to Indian (Pakistani) Cooking'* takes center stage. It involves being open minded and flexible in the kitchen, working with new and interesting ingredients, and shopping in advance for basic Indian staples to cook her delicious recipes at any given time. It also involves learning basic Indian cooking techniques which she clearly illustrates, that can be used to create and then re-create healthy, fresh, easy and delicious home-cooked meals. It involves getting the whole family to take part in the process, whether it's the shopping, peeling carrots, toasting spices, setting the table or doing the dishes, it's all about the team work that takes the drudgery away and makes the whole process something fun.

That's what cooking is all about . . . No matter where your expertise or interest in cooking lies, there's a reason you picked up this book. Obviously you love food, or at least you have an interest in this rich and varied cuisine. Either you want to find out what cooking is all about or you want to pick up a few great new Indian recipes to try out on your friends and family. Maybe you want to spend a little more time in the kitchen and hone your culinary skills. Maybe you want to gain some confidence in the kitchen.

Congratulations! You've come to the right place. This book is filled with food that's exciting, fresh and do-able. And with Farhana's tips and tricks and easy-to-follow techniques, it's easy enough for even the novice. All you'll need is a good set of knives, a stocked Indian/Pakistani pantry, a cutting board, a few bowls and a stove. The rest is all about confidence and taking the time. Let the recipes and pointers that lie between the cover of this book be your guide. Take a deep breath, you can do it!

Joanne Weir

About this Book

Let's blow the whistle on the secrets of Indian/Pakistani cooking

My motive in writing this book is to present a straightforward, uncomplicated, quick and simple way to cook Indian/Pakistani food. And at the same time I want to retain all the authentic flavors, taste and aroma, which is the hallmark of this amazing cuisine.

Through my years teaching primarily Indian/Pakistani cuisine I have seen too many people, (including my children when they had first moved out of the house) caught up in the frustration of certain Indian/Pakistani recipes. Although they were eager to try cooking, they found themselves apprehensive and too intimidated to proceed after seeing a host of unfamiliar ingredients or the tedious steps involved.

I have at times had students, walk into one of my cooking classes holding a certain Indian/Pakistani food recipe they found asking for clarity on a variety of steps or ingredients mentioned in the recipe. I would look at the page long list of a pinch of almost everything under the sun and think to myself, I know this can be simplified. This was the foundation for my approach to my cooking classes from very early on.

I could relate to their frustration, as I had felt it on occasions myself when I had newly moved to the U.S. with my husband and was myself new to cooking. Cooking mainly Indian/Pakistani food at home, the cuisine my husband and I grew up on and relying in those days on a rare Indian cookbook I could lay my hands on to try a recipe that was outside of my collection of family recipes. My goal was to add variation to our family dinners. I remember being overwhelmed just like them by the tiresome list of ingredients. Until one day, I could take it no more, and decided to *rebel* BIG time.

We are at a different time now, where technology *rules* and offers solutions and smoothness to our daily activities everywhere, including the kitchen; and this is America friends and for the most part our kitchens are well equipped. Hallelujah!

So people, let's take advantage of the tools at our disposal. There is no need to seal the pot cover with a layer of dough when steaming 'biryani', like an American student of mine declared having done, employing the authentic '*dampukht*' style of steaming biryani (whatever that is). She had gotten the recipe from an Indian or Pakistani neighbor of hers, who put her to the task. My dear let's step back a bit. Let's slow down and make it easy on ourselves. Just put the lid on the pot and stick it in a 225° oven for a few minutes and you are done. That is my simplified version of the 'biryani' recipe included in this book. So, *please* now, let's not get carried away. I did not have the courage to ask her how long it took her to clean the pot. And by the way, the biryani recipe I'm talking about, gets rave reviews every time I fix it for friends and family.

My learning in simplifying the art of Indian/Pakistani cooking (which continues to be work in progress), came first as a home cook, then as a chef and as owner of a café and catering business, and finally as a cooking instructor for Indian/Pakistani food. Teaching of course pushed me into increasing my own understanding of this cuisine and to look into ways of simplifying it for personal and business use. In addition to my personal experience, I gathered tips and tricks from other chefs and owners of Indian cafes around L.A. who were willing to educate me and share their learning. I have also obtained great ideas from restaurant chefs in Punjab, during my visits to Lahore.

Testing and research

Seeing my expanding interest in learning more about my native cuisine, my family back home through their network of connections, introduced me to the chefs of some well known establishments in Lahore. They would invite me to their kitchens to witness their techniques and, upon my family's request, on occasions would come to our home and give me classes' right there in the kitchen of my parent's home. It pays to have a 'well connected' family-doesn't it? I would in turn take my learning from these experts and put it through my own test kitchen. I would then tweak the ingredients to make a family sized meal and build the recipe for a family-size serving. The research and ground work involved in putting this book together has been a lot of fun and an educational experience for *me*.

My research also took me to local cafes and tandoors. There I have spent many sessions with local experts on the art of making naans, kulfi and 'mathai' (local traditional sweets). It was great fun having them explain and demonstrate to me the step by step method of making some of their specialties.

At our home though, my mother was always the best cook in the house, and a lot of my recipes come from her. Actually both my parents loved to cook, and I remember assisting them on numerous occasions.

Is Indian and Pakistani Cuisine the same?

I say Pakistani/Indian food in the same breath for the fact that until the year 1947 Pakistan and India were one and the same country, so in addition to sharing a similar history the two countries shared the same culture, traditions and of course food. India was divided into two countries, in 1947. India nevertheless is and was then especially a huge country and as my late father, who was at one time in his career a professor of history would always explain it to us, "The country consists of huge rivers flowing through it and in the olden times when means of travel and communication were limited; it created the existence of different languages, customs, traditions and even different cuisines on either banks of these vast rivers".

That perhaps explains, despite the similarities the still amazing uniqueness and varieties of cuisines that exist within different areas and regions of India and Pakistan. And even today when these unique dishes are no longer limited to just their area of origin, it is not unusual for people from one part of the country, to travel to the other part, strictly to enjoy a certain "specialty" of the region. I fondly remember the 'chappli kabobs' of Peshawar. We made many trips to the Northwest frontier part of Pakistan to visit Peshawar dreaming all the way of those moist, luscious 'chappli kabobs' and the Peshawari naans.

And now after my experience with Indian/Pakistani cuisine for over 30 years in the United States, as well as abroad, I see a strong interest internationally and a rapidly growing interest in the United States for the Indian/Pakistani cuisine. This book has been a passion of mine for a long time. I hope it will serve as a valuable source of reference for professional chefs and home cooks alike.

The Myth: 'Indian food is spicy' . . .

Most of the recipes in this book are fairly simple to prepare. Do not let a few unfamiliar ingredients or the use of spices intimidate you or keep you from trying south Asian food.

It is true that Pakistani/Indian food does involve the use of numerous spices, and this stems from the fact that a bulk of the world's spices are grown and cultivated in that part of the world. That is what the voyages of discovery of the 15th and 16th centuries were all about. A search for the spice lands hoping to benefit from the lucrative trade in spices. Back then in Europe and many other countries around the world that lacked in this gift of nature; use of spices was considered a sign of affluence and was a luxury enjoyed by a fortunate few . . .

It was only natural for the Indian cooks at that time to employ the use of these flavorful blessings from a very early period in the world's history. It was actually pretty ingenious and creative of the chefs of that part of the world to employ the clever use of these bounties of nature and take advantage of this wonderful natural resource.

And now the Reality . . .

And yes, Indian/Pakistani food is spicy but that does not necessarily mean 'hot', most spices help make the food more flavorful. The only spice that makes it SPICY meaning 'hot' is cayenne pepper. However, a controlled use of this spice according to your individual preference is going to make the dish only as strong as you would like it to be. The other spices add flavor and aroma to the food, enhance the appetite and make food more fun.

Another significant characteristic and a side benefit of spices is their being a preservative agent. This very practical characteristic of spices makes many of the dishes in the Pakistan/Indian cuisine a great option for a 'do ahead' meal for a party or even for an every day family use. I love the flexibility of fitting this cuisine into our busy lifestyles and it makes it a practical choice for entertaining. Even in Pakistan, this advantage of spices is put to use in spite of the fact that having domestic help is common practice for most households. Some of the dishes come out even more flavorful when the finished product has been allowed to sit for a few hours or overnight in the refrigerator, allowing all the flavors to be fully enhanced. Just as you would make desserts like cheesecake a day or two ahead in order to allow all the flavors to come out stronger, so be bold and daring using these aromatic gifts of nature. Gradually, as you become more familiar with the palate of spices available to you and their use, you will find that you will become more and more at ease and creative in their use in some of your other favorite recipes.

One Last Word . . .

This book has been formulated to blow the cover off the so called *secrets* of Indian/Pakistani cooking, and I am here to let you all know, it may be different- but it's not impossible.

Most of these recipes have gone through my hands many, many times and have successfully passed the taste test with friends, family and business clients.

There is no guess work here, no family secrets held back nor any filler stuff in the pages of this book. What you will find instead is a lot of straightforward directions and techniques shared with a desire to help you enjoy good Indian/ Pakistani food in the comfort of your own home.

So proceed with confidence knowing that with each recipe you are in good hands.

Some tips for using recipes out of this book or from any other source. Read the recipe at least 3-4 times. It is important to picture each step in your mind to get a 'mental picture' of the steps involved. Have all of your ingredients 'prepped' and measured before you start to prepare the dish. So enjoy and keep me posted on your experience in using recipes from this book.

You can e mail me at
Farhana22430@hotmail.com

A Brief Profile and History of Some Spices Used in Pakistani/Indian Cooking

In food spices, spice seeds and herbs are added to lend flavor, aroma and zest. They stimulate appetite, enhance taste and simply delight the gourmet.

Their use throughout history has extended beyond just seasoning food.

The most significant use of spices and herbs in very early times (and even today) has been in medicine. Spices are also utilized as a preservative agent, in cosmetics and even as a textile dye.

They have played an important role in shaping the course of global history, and can be traced to have been a trade commodity between continents as far as 2000 years before the Christian era when the Arabs, the Romans and the Portuguese traded with India and Ceylon for their spices. The spice trade is what led to the famed voyages of discovery of the 15th and 16th century.

Some of the spices used in the Pakistani /Indian cuisine are as follows:

1) Green Cardamom	2) Fenugreek	3) Black Pepper Corns
4) Saffron	5) Red Chili Powder	6) Stick Cinnamon
7) Whole Cloves	8) Coriander	9) Turmeric Powder
10) Cumin /Caraway	11) Fennel Seeds	12) Nigella Seeds
13) Garam Massala	15) Black Cardamom	

Green Cardamom :(Sabz Elaichi)

The green cardamom comes from the family of the ginger plant, the best cardamom grows in the rain forests of southwestern India mainly on the

Malabar coast and in Sri Lanka. Cardamom plantations are work intensive, making the product valuable. Price wise it competes with vanilla for 2nd place behind the most costly of all spices-saffron.

Apart from its uses in curries, rice dishes, Indian/Pakistani puddings and other desserts, cardamom is used in Turkish and Arabic coffee and as an aromatic addition to green and black teas.

Fenugreek (Methi)

In Pakistani/Indian cooking fenugreek (methi) leaves are used in both fresh and dried forms. It is usually added to a dish in its final cooking stage and in small proportions. Methi leaves are highly aromatic and used in the right amount and at the right cooking stage of the dish give the dish a whole new dimension, with spinach and potatoes it is like a marriage made in heaven. It is equally great in some meat dishes.

Black Pepper: (Kali Mirch)

Both the black and the white pepper come from the same plant. The green, red, black and white peppers are simply different stages of ripeness in the little berries of a tropical climbing bush. It is native to India whose Malabar Coast supplies a great deal of the world's pepper. Once ground, the aroma fades fast. So ground pepper is best kept in a sealable container and is best when ground fresh. It is an essential ingredient in the Pakistani/Indian 'garam massala' powder.

Saffron: (Zah-fraan)

From the family of the iris plant some of the best saffron comes from Kashmir. These saffron plantations have existed for ages. The Saffron crocus blooms for two weeks at max. The flowers have to be picked up early in the morning (before it gets too warm) as after that everything wilts. The process of removing the stigma from the flower one blossom at a time is very labor intensive, which contributes to its high price; in addition to the fact that about 150,000 flowers are needed to produce one kilogram of saffron. The bulb starts to bloom two years after planting and after another two years must be dug up, cleaned and replanted. Such efforts and delay make it the most expensive spice in the world. Saffron was used as a medicine as far back as 2600 B.C., and is considered an aphrodisiac.

In Pakistani and Indian cuisine its use ranges from rice dishes, to main dishes and of course those delicious Pakistani/Indian desserts. Its use is generally saved for special guests and fine occasions.

To show my father and his family's extreme desire, affection and respect in asking for my mother's hand in marriage my paternal grandmother wrote a letter to my maternal grandmother using saffron water as ink; as no other medium would have been special enough for this very special lady. And in her acceptance letter my maternal grandmother responded in-kind. Just a bit of family history there!

Red Pepper and Paprika: (Lal Mirch)
There are about ten varieties that exist in the pepper family. Two of which are important as a spice. One is paprika or Spanish pepper. This milder variety is also called 'pimiento'. The other important species and stronger of the two is capsicum frutescent which is used to make cayenne pepper, tabasco and red chili powder. This is the variety used in Pakistani/Indian dishes for its flavor, intensity and rich red color. Personally I prefer using red pepper moderately enough for it to lend some color and a mild intensity to the dish. I use only an amount sufficient to complement the other spices and enhance their aroma, without overpowering them. Over-using this spice in my opinion kills an otherwise flavorful and delicious final product, leaving one sweating, in tears, with a runny nose and gulping down gallons of water. Food, in my 'book' (no pun intended)-should rather be enjoyed not endured.

Stick Cinnamon: (Daar Chini)
Some of the world's finer cinnamon is produced in Sri Lanka (Ceylon) and its known use as a spice and in medicine goes as far back as 2800 B.C.

The bark of cinnamon tree is also used in the cosmetic industry, in liqueur in addition to as a seasoning for food. Waste products from cinnamon are pressed to make cinnamon oil.

The trees grow at sea level up to 700 meters of altitude, and need at least 100 inches of rain every year. The shoots from the plant can be harvested during the rainy season. The bark is loosened with special knives and dried first in the shade and then in the sun.

In Pakistani/Indian cooking cinnamon is used in rice, main dishes and desserts. It is excellent in tea and coffee as well.

Cloves: (Long)

Cloves have been used in the world of medicine for thousands of years. The flower buds of a tree that grows 12 to 15 meters high, can live longer than a century and is most productive at the age of 10-20 years. Each tree is harvested at least four times in a season. Clove buds then must immediately be laid out to dry or else they ferment. Sun drying gives the best results. Its culinary uses in Pakistani/Indian cooking range from curries to biryanis and in many other main dishes; it is used in some dessert dishes as well. It is an essential component of garam-massala and a great mouth freshener.

Coriander: (Dhania)

Though it came to India via Europe coriander is as essential an ingredient in the Indian cuisine as cumin seed or black pepper. Its aromatic green leaves (cilantro) are used not only as a garnish but as an essential herb to flavor many dishes, snacks and chutneys. Its use extends from stove top curries to chutneys. I use it in such abundance in my cooking that my daughters jokingly accuse me of using it even on desserts. Coriander seeds are an essential spice in the Pakistani/Indian spice cabinet both whole and ground.

Turmeric: (Haldi)

This deep yellow spice is such a part of everyday life in Pakistan and India that you find its use in many aspects of the Indian lifestyle, from cooking to cosmetics to medicine and the uses do not end there. It is used as a textile dye and is the main component of many curried dishes. Turmeric is from the ginger family and is the rhizome of the plant. At the time of harvest it is dug up, cooked (by boiling), sun dried for at least a couple of weeks and then cleaned and ground to a fine powder. It favors a tropical climate for its growth. It is very sensitive to sunlight and keeps best when stored in a dark area. Like any other spice it has to be used in just the right amount for best results.

Cumin and Caraway Seeds: (Safaid Zeera/Kala Zeera)

Both of these spices are from the parsley family and do have quite a bit in common, both in texture and aroma. Each has five ridges; both are a shade of brown, with caraway being darker than cumin. In cooking I use cumin more than caraway. This may just be a personal preference and I feel that one could be used instead of the other in flavoring most dishes as the similarities in flavor are strong and often hard to separate. You can differentiate between them however by their color and shape. Where caraway seed has a crescent shape the cumin seed is oval.

Fennel Seeds :(Saunf)

Dry roasted fennel seeds are usually served after dinner as a mouth freshener. The concept is similar to serving an after dinner mint, in addition to being used as an ingredient in the preparation of food, pickles and some desserts. Fennel seeds are also recognized as a digestive aid and a remedy for colic in babies. Fennel water is frequently given to babies in India and Pakistan.

Nigella: (Kalonji)

Nigella (kalonji) is the jet black seeds of a plant which is a variety of the plant called 'love-in-a-mist'. The main use of nigella is in breads and pickles and dishes calling for pickling spices. At Indian /Pakistani markets it is sold under its Indian name 'kalonji'.

Black Cardamom: (Kali Elaichi)
(Some stores or recipes may refer to it as brown cardamom)

Black cardamom is one of the varieties of cardamom. Black cardamom is used mainly in rice and main dishes as opposed to the green cardamom which is used mainly in desserts. It is an essential ingredient of garam massala. In main dishes the black cardamom is used whole. I usually crack it open slightly before adding to the pot so the pod opens up a little and this lets the flavor from its seeds blend in the oil readily and to the dish being cooked.

Garam Massala:

My recipe for garam massala typically is a blend in powder form of the following five spices: cumin seeds, black pepper corns, black cloves, black cardamom and cinnamon. Some commercial varieties of ready made garam massala may have a few more spices blended in addition to the ones listed here.

Garam massala is used mainly as a garnish and a final flavoring on top of a dish just before serving. It is also used in some chutney recipes and is an important ingredient in marinades for grilling chicken and lamb. However, its use should be like most spices in careful quantities as too much of any spice can ruin an otherwise great recipe.

Garam massala can easily be made at home and stored in an airtight jar. Homemade garam massala is usually stronger in flavor and most definitely fresher. It takes only a minute or two to grind it in an electric grinder. I have an extra small container of my blender dedicated to making garam massala powder. It stays in my spice cabinet along with the blender base plugged in and always ready to go. I strongly recommend a similar set up for your kitchen. That is my shortcut to making garam massala in an instant.

(Recipe for garam masala follows)

Author's Note on Spices:

If you have the following spices in your spice cabinet you will be able to fix most of the recipes included in this book and also a good majority of Indian/ Pakistani food recipes in general from any other source.

And these must haves are:

The list for the ground spices includes:	Whole spices you would need:
Coriander power	Cumin seeds
Cumin Powder	Black cloves
Turmeric powder	Black Peppercorns
Cayenne Pepper	Stick cinnamon
Crushed Red Pepper	Black cardamom
Garam Massala	Coriander seeds
Salt	Ajwain
	Nigella

As long as you store them in airtight containers, these spices will remain potent for a long time. Imagine they were carried across the seas in the 15th and 16th century for trade from the Indian sub-continent to Europe and the Western world, where this trip in those days took months or even longer, and they held their potency. In my personal experience I have found them to be quite strong and effective even when they have been stored in my spice cabinet for months, if not years, especially the whole spices.

Garam Massala Recipe

2 tablespoons black pepper corns
1 tablespoon cloves
1" piece of stick cinnamon
2 black cardamoms

Grind all of the above spices together in an electric grinder for a few seconds until finely ground. Store the freshly ground garam massala in an airtight container.

To toast cumin seeds:

Heat a non stick small frying pan and add a teaspoon of cumin seeds to the heated pan. Stir with a wooden spoon for a few seconds, about 15-20 seconds and remove from heat. Continue stirring for even toasting until lightly toasted but not burnt. Transfer the toasted seeds into a bowl or a plate to stop the cooking process. Toasted seeds can be lightly ground using a mortar and pestle, grinding the toasted seeds brings out more of their flavor.

Health Benefits of Herbs and Spices

Being Farhana's husband I have been in the enviable position to enjoy the fruits of her interest and expertise in Pakistani-Indian cooking.

At her core Farhana is an artist. Her artistic creativity, imagination and playfulness add more zest, color, aroma and variety to the already very flavorful, colorful, rich in diversity and delicious Indo-Pak cuisine.

While running her own cafe for several years in the 1990's she developed several original recipes, many of which got quickly in demand. Frequent requests from customers, friends and family for her recipes inspired her teaching, cooking and writing career.

While the focus of Farhana's book is on 'making easy' the preparing and cooking complexity of a foreign though exotic, seductive, mouth-watering and increasingly popular Pakistani-Indian way of making food, I would like to very briefly (in a page) touch on the health benefits of some of the core herbs and spices that make the aromatic curries, tandoori kabobs, and other meat and vegetarian dishes from that part of the world so unique.

Cayenne pepper has capsaicin which is responsible for the 'hotness' of this spice. In Indo-pak meals it also adds visual appeal, unique color and zest. Capsaicin cream has been used topically for years for relief of neuropathic pain. Some of its other reported uses are for weight loss, rhinitis, cluster headaches, fibromyalgia and peripheral circulatory problems. Cayenne peppers are also a source of carotenoids and other micronutrients.

Turmeric, the bright yellow spice ingredient of curries has curcumin as its highly active ingredient. It has been used for a long time (because of its anti-inflammatory properties) for arthritis and some other inflammatory diseases.

It may be of benefit in Alzheimer's disease, in lowering bad cholesterol and in certain types of cancer.

Cinnamon has been used as a carminative and coriander as an appetite stimulant.

Onions may lower our risk of developing certain types of cancer, increase bone density and have anti-inflammatory and antioxidant benefits.

Garlic has anti-clotting, cholesterol and triglyceride reducing and possibly blood pressure reducing properties.

Ginger may help symptoms of gas and abdominal bloating and possibly in reducing symptoms of motion sickness.

While not all reports of benefits are fully supported by unequivocal scientific research, it is clear that herbs and spices do have significant health benefits.

I hope this information adds another dimension to your enjoyment of herb and spice rich recipes in this cookbook.

Afzal Sahibzada MD
DrAfzal.org

Short Cuts and Tips

I love cooking and the value of a home cooked meal. I like having the ability to control my ingredients; knowing exactly where the ingredients came from, how they were handled and the cleanliness behind the prep. An added plus is that it allows you to manage the portion of sodium, sugar, oil, etc. for any diet.

I also desire the task of cooking a meal to be a pleasant one. Cooking is a creative and a mentally relaxing activity that can help one break away from the day's happenings, in other words a helpful stress reducer.

To keep cooking pleasant, fun and positive I like to keep it short and sweet so it does not consume all of an evening. My tips will get you in and out of the kitchen quickly with a delicious, gourmet meal the whole family will enjoy.

Versatility of a Base Curry Sauce in Indian Cooking:
Employing the similarity of base sauce in curry based recipes as a time saving tool

As you gain more familiarity with Indian/Pakistani cuisine, you will find that most curry dishes have the same or similar base sauce. Especially poultry and meat curries, some of the examples are chicken curry, kofta curry (meatball curry), Aloo gosht, etc.

Since the base sauce prep is similar in a lot of curry dishes that are part of Indian/Pakistani cuisine, a good short cut is to have a few batches prepared and frozen in an airtight container for future use. My mother lived in Lahore, Pakistan and was fortunate to have domestic help available to run the home. Even though she had a cook to prepare the family meals, she still made sure her freezer was well stocked with multiple batches of curry base. This trick saved her many times when unexpected company dropped by, or the family cook was out of commission for any reason. She was a very practical woman and always believed in planning ahead.

A well known practice in many Indian/Pakistani homes is to divide cooking time into two days, as once you have a batch of already prepared curry saved in the refrigerator or the freezer, all you have to do is add meat or vegetables to it. This practice can allow you to have the dinner ready in half the time of starting it from a scratch. Another short cut is to have a big batch of onions sautéed and ready in the refrigerator. Onions sautéed in advance come in handy in cooking many vegetarian or meat dishes included in this book.

Set aside a day for cooking to last a week or more.

If you don't mind leftovers, investing some hours one day in cooking a couple of dishes, and refrigerating them for use during the week can spare a few evenings of cooking. And best of all dinner is ready as soon as you come home.

I use this aspect of Indo/Pakistani recipes a lot in my favor and for my sanity. Then the act of cooking remains a pleasant and a fun one. I might add a quick vegetable dish or a salad to bring a little variety to my leftovers-I have friends who have this art down so well, they boast of cooking enough for a month or so and have their freezer packed to last a while. I may have occasionally done that, but I enjoy cooking more often. Also a part of the weekend could be utilized to cook for the whole week ahead.

Team Work

I bring this up in my cooking classes and I strongly believe in it—"Make it a family affair." As far as I am concerned, the real *aphrodisiac* is not in the ingredients, it is in the act of 'sharing and caring'. Pitching in can be in so many forms; picking up stuff from the market, laying the table, throwing out the trash, cleaning up after, etc. My Swedish friend Christina Elmrose, a lover of Indian food, started the tradition of us planning an evening of cooking together for our families once a month when we spent some years together in the middle east in the 80's. We developed a close friendship fast. I carried the ritual over to my family back home and would get everyone involved in doing fun cooking together. If you've never done it, try it-you'll love it.

Working with a New Recipe:

Look, whenever you are starting with a new recipe, whether you are new to cooking or experienced, there are several steps you must take to get a good handle on your new project. Set aside a minute to read and re-read the recipe. In addition to working with a new recipe, I do this also when I am coming back to a recipe that I have not worked with for a while. Try to envision every step in your mind's eye, make your own notes; convince yourself that you are in charge of the recipe. Then, as you do the prep, start with assembling all of the ingredients listed for that particular recipe. Cooking then, is a breeze and you won't find that you're running ahead of yourself or playing catch up going back and forth from the pot to the cutting board.

Time saving kitchen tools

A Sharp Knife:

This may sound very basic but it is very, very important. First and foremost you need a sharp knife. A really sharp knife that feels right in your hands and is easy for you to handle and work with. You'd be surprised how much of a time saver the right knife is when it comes to cutting meat and vegetables. So definitely invest in a couple of good knives and make sure they are very sharp you'll be glad you did.

A Food Processor or Chopper:

A food processor in the kitchen is a must. It could be a small well working hand held mini chopper, a slightly larger food processor or a blender, any one of these will cut down a lot on the cooking time by speeding up the steps. Using a food processor to puree tomatoes in tomato based curries for example, will help in cutting down a lot of labor and time involved in the curry prep. An Indian kitchen will also usually have a nice batch of ginger and garlic pureed and stored in the refrigerator.

Food processor

With a processor or a hand held chopper it's pureed in seconds.

A Heavy Cleaver:

A cleaver or a heavy duty knife is handy to cut up meat with bones, if at anytime you are dealing with cutting up a whole chicken or any other meat with bones. Please use extra care and caution in using any of these kitchen tools and gadgets, and protect yourself at all times.

A kitchen meat cleaver

A Lemon Peel Grater

A lemon grater is a must in the kitchen and is really handy to grate lemon peel, ginger root or any other ingredient needed for a recipe. It is another time saving tool in the kitchen.

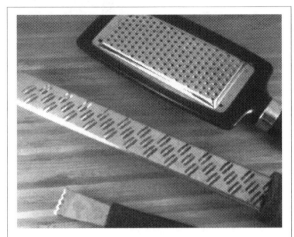

A collection of lemon graters

A Vegetable Slicer

This is a life saver to slice or julienne ginger, carrots, cucumbers or any other vegetable. It will do all of the above in seconds and saves a whole lot of time and effort in the kitchen. Check with a kitchen ware store and they will be more than happy to guide you to buy a good vegetable slicer.

One of my favorite tools in the kitchen, this slicer comes with a variety of slicing plates and a vegetable holder to protect the hands

A GUIDE TO THE CURRY PREP
(or the 'base sauce' prep)

Some Key Steps to Cooking an Indian curry

The following tips are a guide to ensure good results even at the very first attempt at a new curry recipe. You can apply these tips to any curry recipe in this book, or an Indian curry recipe you may have found elsewhere

Sautéing onions:

As I had mentioned earlier, most vegetarian and non-vegetarian curries in Indian/Pakistani cooking start with the sautéing of onions until they start to turn a very light gold or a soft brown in color. When working on sautéing the onions, stir the onions, stir them often as you sauté them. You need to do that to ensure an even cooking and browning of onions, and also to avoid any accidental charring of even a single strand of the sliced onion. A burnt piece of onion will lend a burnt flavor to the whole pot and make it impossible to salvage the final outcome from the color or odor of the charred piece.

In most of my recipes I sauté the onions to the point where most of the water from the onions has evaporated, and they have just started to look translucent and have begun to turn a very light golden brown at the edges. I will then proceed to the next step, avoiding any chance of charring even a single strand.

Tips in sautéing spices for the base curry sauce:

These tips apply to most curry based dishes in Indian cooking, and demand the same caution and attention as the steps mentioned prior for browning onions. A little attention to detail here will help you produce results like a pro. Trust me; there is no gimmick to Indian/Pakistani cooking. It is simple and easy to master and that's what this book is about.

It is required in most vegetarian and non vegetarian dishes to sauté all the spices, to remove their raw edge and to help bring out their aroma. It involves cooking these spices on a relatively high heat. If the spice and onion mixture dries up too much, the recipe will usually direct you to add a few tablespoons of water and sauté some more. It may ask you to repeat this step a few times over the next 7 to 10 minutes.

This step in the making of a curry sauce is a crucial one, and some investment in hands on attention here will pay huge dividends down the road. My recipes outline these instructions under 'directions'. I am including them here again merely as a reminder to employ these steps as the recipe suggests, so that you will be happy with the outcome.

I am hoping you will find this information helpful as you prepare an Indian curry dish, and it helps you gain better control over your recipes as you venture into this cuisine.

Different stages of base sauce in curried dishes

OK, Where Do I start?

New to Cooking or New to Indian/Pakistani Cooking

Let's say you are someone who is new to cooking, and have not done much cooking before, but would like to now increase your confidence and skill levels in this area, or you are an experienced cook but have never tried Indian or Pakistani cooking before, so this short bit of information is carefully put together just for you.

Believe me I have been there so I know well the challenges of a new cook.

It's the fear of the outcome, in a nutshell.

You name it and I have done it, ruined recipes in many ways and got discouraged about future attempts. There have been times when I have burnt them (on a second thought, I have not totally given up on that), on other occasions thought I had followed the recipe precisely and still not completely satisfied with the outcome, thrown out pots because it was too much work to scrape off the burnt residue at the bottom, and the list goes on . . .

Over time I have learnt that it is easier to make it right the first time and way more difficult to ruin an end product. Yes, you heard me right; cooking a good meal is way easier than ruining a good recipe. Look, you ruin a recipe and the work is now doubled . . . why? Well you have to start all over again, and now it's costing you more effort and time.

No, all kidding aside, seriously I am going to suggest good recipes to start out with, to ease into this cuisine with some simpler entrées. Start by taking some baby steps, if you will, and then slowly work your way into those recipes that seem more involved. If you choose to go this route and start with these suggested recipes, make them a few times over to build your confidence in

xlix

the kitchen and with this cuisine. This will greatly increase your familiarity with the use of spices and the steps of cooking involved, and believe me you will soon be making adjustments and amendments to these recipes for your own particular palette.

So here are some of the recipes I would start out with:

1:    Chicken Karahi, p 86
2:    A Quick Chicken Massala Stir Fry: serves two, p 100
3:    Aloo (Palak) Methi, p 39
4:    Vegetable Raita or Cucumber Raita, pgs 29/36
5:    Boiled Rice with Vegetables, p 159
6:    Sooji Halwa (dessert), p 187

By no means am I suggesting to totally limiting yourself to the list above, if you come across any other recipe that seems easy enough as you read it go for it.

The last item I would put on that list is:

7:    'A take charge attitude', and that is the most important place to start, with a full force 'Yes I Can Do It" attitude, as I often tell myself: 'Farhana you control the recipe, the recipe does not control you, you are in charge here and you will make it happen!'

To have a better command of the recipe, read it a few times, try to envision every step in your mind's eye and try to get a clearer picture of it for yourself; and then focus on a prep, that will make your efforts and life easier.

Do all the cutting, chopping, slicing, washing, draining and measuring of ingredients in play before you start the actual cooking. On occasions if I am in a hurry to be in and out of the kitchen fast, even I think I can break this rule and sometimes I do and it only adds to my frustration. So trust me, this will make you feel like a pro in the kitchen. Like a chef on TV, you see how they can make everything look so easy . . . it's all in the prep.

I would love to hear of your success stories, and even any challenges you may encounter as you start to use the recipes from this book. This would allow me to help you better to tweak the steps or directions. Do assist me with your feed back, and enjoy the process as you include these recipes in your home cooking. As a neighbor of mine once called it, (home-cooked) *'it's the best take out!'*

Indian/Pakistani Street Foods and Snacks!

Street food vendors are a familiar part of the Pakistani/Indian street scene and lifestyle.

Growing up there you become accustomed to their presence from an early age. These street vendors are waiting for you with their colorful and tantalizing snacks as you are let out of school or at the street corner as you are approaching home. They would pass by your neighborhood riding their bikes loaded with goodies, and lure you over with their chant.

Bringing in snacks like papadums (or papar), daal murmura, kulfi, spicy corn on the cob and a variety of fresh toasted nuts, including pine nuts, peanuts and more.

It would always amaze me how those gigantic wafer thin stacks of papadums layered carefully in his wire rack would stay put and keep from cracking. And as soon as you bought one he was sure to hand you over a picture perfect treat.

But that is not where their popularity ends, no that is just the beginning . . . from the street corner they would just as gladly make their way to the most sophisticated of affairs, offered with delight at the most formal of party spreads. The presentations may be different and up scaled, but the core of the snack remains the same.

I remember many years back traveling with both my daughters when they were just two and five, finding myself in an eight hour transit at London's Heathrow airport. I couldn't be very mobile with two young kids who were catching up on their sleep after the first leg of our journey and were spread over the airport seats, but to my delight I found an airport café just across from where my kids were napping, selling one of my favorite snacks 'the Samosa'. You can only imagine how pleased I was, as thanks to these samosas, this turned out to be the shortest eight hours I ever had to spend in transit. The samosas and I connected quickly, and I felt right at home. I don't know how those samosas did at this café on other days, but on that particular day they definitely had an awesome selling day, as even the calorie count was not holding me back.

Following are recipes for some common street foods, they make excellent snacks and appetizers.

Pakoras

Enjoyed best, and are totally addictive, when these crisp and crunchy snacks are served hot out of the fryer . . . Perfect with mint, tomato or tamarind chutney (or even tomato ketchup) these snacks are a must with a cup of tea on a rainy afternoon or anytime friends and family gather to spend some time together.

- 1 cup chickpea flour
- 2 teaspoons rice flour (optional)
- 1 teaspoon salt (or to taste)
- ½ teaspoon dried fenugreek leaves (Kasoori methi-available at Indian/Pakistani spice stores)if readily available
- ½ teaspoon cumin seeds
- ½ teaspoon cayenne pepper
- 1/2 teaspoon crushed red pepper
- ½ teaspoon coriander seeds, lightly crushed
- ½ teaspoon pomegranate seeds* (whole or ground) *available at Indian/Pakistani spice stores
- ¼ teaspoon baking powder
- 1/4 cup loosely packed, chopped cilantro
- 1/4 cup chopped green onions
- 2 teaspoons green chilies, seeded and finely chopped
- about 1 cup of cold water, or enough to make a smooth batter
- 1 medium white potato, thin sliced
- 1 cup fresh spinach leaves
- 1 medium onion peeled and cut into thin rings
- Vegetable oil for deep-frying

YIELD: 2 dozen large or 3 dozen medium pakoras

1. Combine the two flours, salt, fenugreek leaves, cumin seeds, cayenne pepper, crushed red pepper, coriander seeds, pomegranate seeds

and baking powder in a bowl. Add the chopped cilantro and green onions. Mix well with a wire whisk or a spoon.

2. Slowly add cold water while whisking the batter until it achieves the consistency of medium-light cream. The batter should be thick enough to coat the vegetables well. Let the batter sit for a few minutes.

3. Fold the prepared vegetables into the batter.

4. Pour oil, to the depth of 6.5-7.5 cm (2-3 inches), in a wok or deep-fryer until the temperature reaches about 350° degrees F.

5. Drop batter coated vegetable pieces with some extra batter into the hot oil by the spoonfuls (6-8 at a time). Fry on each sides for a minute or two, until they turn a light golden brown on both sides.

6. Remove with a slotted spoon and drain on paper towels.

Continue cooking until all the pakoras are done. Serve while warm with chutney or equally good with ketchup.

Serves 8-12

Samosas

A very popular street food of India and Pakistan, the "Samosa" has more recently gained a global identity. My contribution in boosting that identity locally was in selling 'samosa platters' at my café in Woodland Hills, California. Samosas are popular and delicious, both with vegetable and meat fillings. They are great as a snack or an appetizer, or as part of a main meal. Whether you find it on the platter of a street vendor in Delhi or Lahore, on the menu of a fine restaurant or at the coffee shop of a busy airport . . . the samosa holds it's own in flavor and zest.

Deep frying the samosas in vegetable oil

For the filling
- 6 medium potatoes (Russet)
- (Boiled in a pot of water with skin on)
- ½ teaspoon *Garam Massala*
- 1 teaspoon salt, or to taste
- ½ teaspoon crushed red pepper
- ¼ teaspoon cumin seeds
- A pinch of ajwain
- ¼ teaspoon coarsely ground coriander seeds
- ½ bunch cilantro finely chopped
- 1 bunch green onions, chopped finely
- 2 Serrano chilies seeded and finely chopped
- 1 cup peas
- a pinch of salt
- 1 tablespoon vegetable oil

■ Let the potatoes cool down to a workable temperature, and while still quite warm, peel off the skins, put the peeled potatoes in a deep bowl and coarsely mash with a fork to the consistency of scrambled eggs. Mix in the dry spices the salt, crushed red pepper, coriander seeds, ajwain, garam massala and the cumin seeds into the warm and the coarsely mashed potatoes, adjust seasoning to taste.

- Fold in half of the chopped cilantro, green onions and the green chilies to the potatoes. Potatoes absorb flavors from seasonings and herbs readily while still warm, it is important to add the spices and herbs to potatoes before they cool down completely.

- Heat oil in an open frying pan; add the remaining chopped green onions, cilantro, green chilies and the peas with a pinch of salt and sauté for 2 minutes. Add the sautéed peas to the seasoned potatoes and mix well.

Wrapping and Frying the Samosas:

Using Store Bought Wrappers:
1 Package of Spring Roll/Egg roll Wrappers (Available at most oriental food markets)

For the Sealing Paste:
1 egg white beaten
4-6 teaspoons plain flour

Start out by mixing 4 teaspoons of flour into the egg white in a small bowl with a spoon, mix the flour well to reach the consistency of a thick paste. Add more flour if needed. If the paste is too thin it will not seal the wrappers securely.

Start to work with one rectangle piece at a time. Separate sheets holding them at the edge, and picking up 2 layers at a time.

Forming Samosas Using the Egg Roll Wrapper:

The egg roll wrapper sheets come in a square. Cut the square into 3 equal rectangles. Start tearing off egg roll wrappers from each rectangle, picking up two layers at a time

Starting at one end of the separated piece fold the sheet to form a cone, hold the triangular cone shape in place and seal it with the sealing paste so it holds its form. At this point there should be a portion of the sheet remaining and sticking above the wider opening of the cone cavity. Fill the cavity with the filling, cover the top opening with the extended portion of the sheet and seal the flap using the prepared sealing paste. Deep fry in oil heated to about 400° (F) until the wrapping turns a light golden brown.

Drain on paper towels and serve warm with chutney.

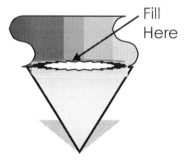

Fill
Here

HOMEMADE SAMOSA WRAPPERS VERSION II:

Teaching a Samosa Making Class in Santa Monica, California to Culinary Students at the Art's Institute.

- 2 ½ cups all-purpose flour
- Salt
- Ajwain one generous pinch
- Cumin seeds one generous pinch
- ¼ cup vegetable oil
- ½ cup water

■ Mix all of the dry ingredients in a bowl or container of a food processor, add the oil and mix until the oil is well incorporated. Add half of the measured water and continue mixing. Gradually add the remaining ¼ cup water as you continue to mix. Add more water if needed, 2 tablespoons at a time up to another ¼ cup. Process until combined. Transfer combined dough on to a work surface.

■ The dough should be workable but firm. Knead for a few minutes, form a large dough ball and set it in a bowl, cover with plastic or a moist towel until ready to use. Let the dough ball rest at room temperature for 25-30 minutes before using; divide the dough into two equal portions.

■ Take one portion and roll into a log and cut the log into 8-10 equal portions with a knife. Using your fingers flatten each piece slightly. With a rolling pin start to roll out each flattened piece to form an oval thin shape about 6 inches long and 3 to 4 inches wide in the widest part in the middle. Cut each oval piece in the middle, each piece will yield two samosas.

- Overlap the cut end to form a cone, hold cone in place by moistening the dough at the crease. Fill the cavity of the cone with the filling, and seal the opening by moistening the dough at the outer edge of the opening to form the samosa. Deep fry in medium hot oil (350°) until golden on all sides, fry in batches of 6-8.

Serve with tamarind and/or mint chutney.

Filling Samosas:

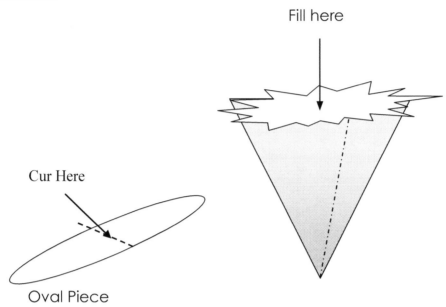

Fill here

Cur Here

Oval Piece

Behl Poori

This fun "street snack' can be offered at coffee mornings with friends, as a salad or enjoyed as an 'anytime' snack. It is quick and easy to fix.

Main Filling:
- 4 medium potatoes peeled and diced into small cubes.
- ½ teaspoon salt
- 2 cups puffed rice (available at Indian food stores)
- 1 cup Sev (available at Indian food stores)
- 1 dozen pappri (mini crisp pooris available at Indian food stores)
- 1 teaspoon toasted cumin seeds (see p. 215)
- 1 16oz can of chick peas (garbanzo beans) drained
- ½ an onion chopped and marinated in 4 tablespoons of fresh lemon juice (optional)

Topping:
- ½ cup yogurt blended smooth with ½ cup milk
- 2 dozen pappri (pooris)
- 1 cup tamarind chutney
- 1 cup plum chutney
- 1 cup mint chutney
  (See chutney recipes under: 'Chutneys, Raitas and Condiments')

Garnish:
- Fresh chopped cilantro
- 1 chopped tomato
- 1 diced banana
- 1 diced apple

For the Garnish:

Mix all of the ingredients for the garnish in a small bowl and set aside.

For the main filling:

Boil the potatoes for 7-12 minutes with the ½ teaspoon of salt, until tender. Drain in a colander. Place the store bought puffed rice in a mixing bowl and add the sev. Crush the pappri (pooris) and add to the mix in the bowl. Add the potatoes, chick peas, cumin seeds and the chopped onion and mix well. (Instead of mixing in the bowl, the chopped onion can be used as topping on each individual serving)

To Serve:

Pour a serving of the main filling mix (about ½ cup) into an individual serving bowl, top with a couple of spoonfuls of the blended yogurt pour the chutneys on top, garnish with a tablespoon or two of the garnish mix and sprinkle more crushed pappri (pooris) on top and serve.

Serves 8-10

Aloo Channay Pappri Chaat

from Bano Bazzar

When I was growing up in Punjab samosas, pakoras and fruit chaat were the snacks that we craved, as opposed to candy, chocolate or chips. I remember, so often a group of us friends would sneak out of college in between classes and go all the way to Lahore's "*Bano bazaar*" to our favorite chaat house especially for their fruit chaat. So you can imagine my excitement when more recently some of the Indian spice stores in L.A. started serving those same street favorites. I am lucky to have one such store close to my home in the valley, and it is a favorite stop with us for an afternoon snack with a cup of *chai* (tea).

For the main filling

- 4 medium sized potatoes, peeled, diced, boiled, drained and allowed to cool.
- 1-16 oz. can garbanzo beans, drained and washed
- 1 large granny smith apple diced, given a quick lemon water bath* and drained
- 1 large tomato diced
- 2 tablespoons chopped onion
- 2 bananas sliced, given a quick lemon water bath* and drained
- 4 tablespoons chopped cilantro

*Lemon water bath:

Squeeze juice from one lemon in a bowl and add one cup cold water to it, soak the diced apples in for a quick bath and take them out with a slotted spoon. Repeat for bananas, this will keep these fruits from discoloration.

Gently fold all of the ingredients in a bowl and chill until ready to serve.

Yogurt Topping:

- 3 cups yogurt, well blended
- 4 tablespoons chopped cilantro

- 4 tablespoons finely chopped onion
- 1 teaspoon toasted cumin (see p. 215)
- ¼ teaspoon ground black pepper
- ½ teaspoon salt
- 4 tablespoons sugar
- ¼ cup chopped cucumber

Directions: for yogurt topping

Mix all of the above ingredients and chill until ready to serve.

Tamarind Chutney for Dressing:
See recipe for tamarind chutney under Chutneys and Condiments

Garnish:
Store bought 'Pappri' or *papdi* (available at most Indian spice stores, pappri is deep fried mini pooris used to add a crisp topping to the chaat) if pappri is not readily available, deep fried pita chips or deep fried flour tortillas pieces could work as a substitute topping.

1 lettuce head, with the leaves separated to serve the chaat in individual servings (optional)

To Serve: (For Individual Servings)

Line the individual serving bowl with a lettuce leaf; fill the leaf with a few spoonfuls of the main fruit and vegetable filling, top with a few spoonfuls of the blended yogurt sauce. Break the Pappri into smaller pieces and sprinkle on top of the yogurt along with the toasted ground cumin and the tamarind chutney. Top with a portion of the garnish mix as desired.

Serve with extra chutneys on the side.

Serves 8-10

The Traditional Fruit Chaat

Nature blessed in abundance the Indo/Pakistan sub-continent with the wonderful natural resource of spices, and I must say people there made Mother Nature *proud* by putting this natural resource to good creative use. And for me, here is another example of this ingenuity: dressing up the fruit salad like no one can, and the end result is kicking up nature's candy to unmatched levels of 'delight'. Who needs those sugar loaded sweets when there is fruit chaat to share, healthy, nutritious and delicious. Serve it at your next brunch or coffee morning, and you will find them licking their spoons. You can pretty much go for any fruit you like. This recipe is built around the following selection:

Fruit
- 2 large mangoes peeled and diced
- 1 apple diced
  (then given a quick lemon water bath* and drained)
- 2 bananas sliced in thick rounds
  (then given a quick lemon water bath* and drained)
- 2 cups grapes
- 1 cup or more of sliced strawberries
- 1 guava (if readily available in the market)
- 2 cups diced Mexican papaya
- 1 orange cut in thick chunks

*Lemon water bath:
Squeeze juice from one lemon in a bowl and add one cup cold water to it, put the diced apples in the lemon water for a quick bath and take them out with a slotted spoon. Repeat for bananas, this will keep the fruits from discoloration.

Dressing:
- 1cup orange juice
- juice of 1 lemon
- ½ teaspoon cumin seeds (toasted*, if desired)
- ½ teaspoon crushed red pepper
- ½ teaspoon salt
- 6 tablespoons sugar
- ½ teaspoon chaat massala (available at Indian spice stores)

To toast cumin: heat a small frying pan and add cumin seeds to the pan. Stir with a wooden spoon for an even and uniform toasting and to keep the seeds from over cooking or burning. About 1-2 minutes. Remove from heat, if desired lightly grind using a mortar and pestle. Cumin aroma kicks up when toasted.

Combine all of the ingredients in a bowl, stir with a spoon to blend well. Adjust for the sugar and salt balance to taste. Set aside.

Add all of the prepared fruit into a mixing bowl. Pour the prepared dressing over the fruit and gently fold the fruit in the dressing. Transfer the fruit chaat to a serving bowl and serve.

Serves 8-10

Dahee Baray

(Quickly deep fried lentil fritters with yogurt topping) (AKA:Dahee Bhallay)

I have added my own variations to this popular snack and street food both in ingredients and in the method of cooking. Then I put my version to the test in several of my cooking classes and it has tested strong. I hope it will get your vote of confidence as well. In my version below, I have added some herbs and spices to the batter just to add more flavors, and occasionally I will eliminate the step of soaking the fried fritter in water, and that keeps the fritter crisp.

For the Barras (fritters):
- ½ cup moong daal (urad)
- ½ cup maash daal
  (Both daals soaked in water for 2-4 hours or even an overnight. If soaking for an overnight keep in the refrigerator)
- Salt to taste
- ¾ teaspoon baking soda
- ½ teaspoon pureed ginger
- ½ teaspoon pureed garlic
- ¼ cup chopped Cilantro
- ¼ cup chopped green onion
- 2 Serrano chilies seeded and finely chopped
- ½ teaspoon toasted ground cumin*
- ¼ teaspoon cayenne pepper
- Oil for deep frying
- A deep bowl filled with water at room temperature to soak the fried fritters

* see directions to toast cumin seeds under chapter on spices

Drain the daals and grind them together to a smooth paste in a food processor with the salt, baking soda and the ginger and garlic puree.

17

Transfer contents of the food processor into a mixing bowl—add the chopped cilantro, green onions, Serrano chilies, ground cumin and ground red pepper to the daal mixture, mix well with a spoon.

Heat oil in a deep frying pan or a deep fryer to 350° F, gently drop batter by tablespoons full in the heated oil, fry on both sides. Lower heat if oil seems too hot. The fritters should cook evenly and thoroughly so adjust the temperature for even cooking. Drain the fried dumplings on a paper towel and immediately add them to the bowl of room temperature water. Leave in the water for about five minutes and then take each fritter and squeeze out excess water by pressing them between the palms of your hands, then place them in a serving bowl.
(If you prefer crispier dumplings omit the step of soaking them in water)

Pour yogurt sauce over the fried fritters and garnish with chopped tomato and cilantro. Sprinkle ground cumin and paprika or chaat massala (available in most Indian spice stores) and serve with tamarind and plum chutneys.

For the yogurt topping:
- 2 cups yogurt
- ¼ cup milk
- 1 teaspoon toasted whole cumin
- ¼ teaspoon crushed red pepper toasted and ground
- 4 tablespoons sugar
- ½ teaspoon salt

- ½ teaspoon chaat massala

Mix all of the above ingredients, making sure the yogurt is blended smooth. Pour over the fritters, garnish and serve with the chutneys.

Garnish: Chopped tomato, cilantro, toasted cumin (finely ground) and chaat massala.

Yield: 10-12 fritters

Chicken Shammi Kabobs

Shammi Kabobs are traditionally made with lamb or beef. The meat from the leg of lamb is the best portion to use, or any stewing beef available at the market. They can also be made with chicken. My version here is a combination of beef and chicken, with chicken as the dominant portion of the two meats in play. I use chicken thighs, as thighs have a good amount of moisture resulting in a moist kabob. Kabobs make great leftovers, and leftover kabob patties can be frozen in zip lock bags or any air tight container for later use.

FOR STEP ONE:

- 8 chicken thighs
- skin removed, fat trimmed and washed
- 1 lb. stewing beef or lamb
- 2/3 cup 'channa daal' (lentils)
- 3 cloves of garlic
- 1 teaspoon of pepper corns
- 2 black cardamoms slightly pounded to crack open
- 1 teaspoon cumin seeds
- 1 teaspoon salt
- 4 cups water

Mix all of the above ingredients in a deep pot and cook over a medium flame until most of the water in the pan has evaporated, but not completely dry. The meat should be well cooked and tender, where it easily splits apart with the stirring spoon and the lentils (channa daal) are completely cooked and tender, and mash at the touch. (approximate cooking time 1-1 ½ hours). When about ¾ of the water has evaporated, uncover the pot, lower the flame and simmer for another few minutes. Keep an eye as you simmer not to let the mix over-dry. The mix should have slight moisture bubbling around the edges when you turn the flame off. Cover the pot and let it sit for a few minutes before the next step.

TOOLS FOR STEP TWO:

- A food processor
- A Spatula or cooking spoon

Step Two:
Transfer the cooked mixture in batches into the food processor and do a quick puree to blend well. Transfer the pureed mixture into a large mixing bowl.

FOR STEP THREE:
- 1 bunch green onions finely chopped
- 2 Serrano chilies seeded and finely chopped
- ½ bunch cilantro finely chopped (stems and leaves together)
- 2 tablespoons of fresh ginger finely chopped or slivered
- ½ teaspoon garam massala
- 1 teaspoon salt or to taste
- ¼ teaspoon crushed red pepper (optional)
- the pureed mix

Step Three:
Mix all of the above ingredients to the consistency of pliable dough. If the mix seems too dry for a workable consistency then add one egg and a few drops of water. The consistency of the mix should allow you to form patties with ease and without the mix crumbling up as you form patties. With clean hands take small amounts of the mix and aided with small amounts of cold water on your finger tips form small patties (1 ½" to 2"). The mix should yield between 25-30 patties. (formed meat patties can be stored in the freezer in zip lock bags or plastic containers and fried later)

FOR STEP FOUR:
- Oil for frying Kabobs (meat patties)

For Step Four:

Heat oil in a frying pan to a nice 350 ° and fry patties, a couple of minutes on each side till the patties are nicely browned. If the oil is not heated to the needed temperature the patties will start to break. Drain on a plate lined with a double layer of paper towels.

Serve with mint chutney, ketchup or a dressing of your choice.

To fry leftover kabobs stored in the freezer, take them out of the freezer about ½ an hour before frying, or let them sit in the refrigerator for a few hours to thaw. Fry using the same steps mentioned above.

Yield: about 18-20 kabobs

Chutneys, Raitas
and
Other Condiments

Like most cuisines of the world, Indian/Pakistani food has its own share of delightful condiments in limitless varieties, designed to enhance the flavors of appetizers, snacks and meals. Quick to fix, some of these condiments can last in your refrigerator for days.

Correspondingly, as is true for many recipes in various cuisines of the world, you will see a range of different recipes for the same dish in the Indo/Pak cuisine as well. Mint Chutney is one example of this however, the different options for mint chutney recipes will have some similarity of ingredients. If nothing else, as far as mint chutneys go-all mint chutneys come in a shade of green. The green color comes from the ingredients used for example, mint, green chili and cilantro, and sometimes a certain variation may even call for raw mango (again green) for tartness.

Whichever mint chutney recipe you opt for, please DO NOT use the one that calls for using 'green' food color . . . stay away from the 'imposter' recipe. I am just trying to infuse some fun here as not too long ago I happened to stop by a local spice store to pick up some samosas for lunch, and the chutney this nice place packed had actual food coloring in it, the samosas nevertheless were good. Food color in mint chutney was certainly a first for me.

I have included a selection of some of the popular condiment recipes in this section, and hope you have fun preparing them and sharing them with friends and family.

Mint Chutney

Chutneys in general are a great addition on the side to any Indian dish, and mint chutney is one of the more popular ones for daily meals. It is especially great with deep fried snacks, appetizers and grilled food. See also the mint chutney raita dressing recipe that follows. The 'raita dressing' uses mint chutney as one of its main ingredient. I originally developed this variation to the mint chutney to serve with samosas and other Indian snacks offered at my café.

- ½ bunch fresh cilantro
- ½ bunch fresh mint
- 1 whole Serrano chili, stem removed
- 1 teaspoon pomegranate seeds
- 3 cloves of garlic
- ½ onion chopped
- ½ teaspoon salt
- ¼ cup lemon juice
- 3 tablespoons sugar

For Chutney:

Blend all of the ingredients listed above in a blender or a food processor for 30 to 40 seconds until blended well. Mint chutney can be stored in the refrigerator for up to two weeks when stored in an airtight container with a firm lid.

Mint Chutney Raita/Dressing

This raita works as a great salad dressing and as a dip for vegetables. For a thicker and a richer consistency add both the mayonnaise and sour cream. The proportions of ingredients here can be adjusted to your specific preference; however, the version below will yield a good variation.

- 1 cup mint chutney
- (Prepared according to the recipe in this book)
- 1 cup yogurt
- ¼ cup mayonnaise or sour cream
- ½ teaspoon toasted and then ground cumin seeds (p.215)
- 1 tablespoon dried dill weed or 2 tablespoons of chopped fresh dill
- ¼ cup olive or vegetable oil

For Raita Dressing:

Mix the prepared chutney with yogurt, mayonnaise or sour cream, and the toasted and ground cumin seeds, dill weed and oil and blend well with a spoon. Adjust the balance of sugar and salt to taste. Season the dressing with fresh ground black pepper, if desired.

The dressing can be stored in the refrigerator in an airtight container for up to 2 weeks.

Plum Chutney

My version of plum chutney is great with snacks and appetizers included in this book, and works as another fruity and flavorful homemade salad dressing. Another 'quick to fix' condiment, the end product results in a vibrant and rich deep red color. Plum chutney can be stored in the refrigerator in an airtight container for up to two weeks.

- 3 medium sized plums pureed
- ½ cup lemon juice
- ½ cup water
- 1½ cup sugar
- ¾ teaspoon salt
- ¼ teaspoon cayenne pepper
- 1 teaspoon cumin seeds lightly toasted and ground (p.215)

Mix all of the above ingredients, except for the sugar, in a saucepan and cook over a medium flame for about five minutes. Stir as it boils; add sugar and continue cooking for another 7 to 8 minutes until the mixture thickens to the thickness of an egg white. Cool completely and serve with Samosas, pakoras or as a topping for fruit chaat.

This chutney works great as a topping for salads as well.

Tamarind Chutney

(Imli Chutney)

During one of my cooking classes when we served this chutney with the snacks we had prepared to go with it, a student, as she took the first taste remarked, "I could drink it with a straw!" Occasionally I mix it with yogurt and pour it on my salads, or dip fresh cut vegetables in it. It is also great with deep fried appetizers like samosas and pakoras, and as a topping with snacks like fruit chaat (p.15) and dahee baray (p.17).

- 2 tablespoons tamarind paste
- 1 teaspoon salt
- 1 ½ cups sugar
- I teaspoon garam massala
- 3 cups water
- ½ teaspoon ground red pepper
- 2" piece Mexican raw sugar *(piloncillo)* or Indian raw sugar, AKA: *gur*
- or ½ cup brown sugar
- ½ teaspoon toasted and coarsely ground cumin (p.215)

Combine all of the above ingredients in a heavy bottom saucepan and cook over a medium low flame, stirring occasionally. Cook for 35-45 minutes, then cool completely. The sauce will appear thinner and runny when hot but will thicken as it cools. Tamarind chutney is great with Samosas, on salads and with many other Indian and Pakistani snacks and appetizers.

Yogurt Raita

Variations to this recipe are only limited to one's imagination and taste buds. Here is a version I get good reviews on.

* To toast cumin seeds: Heat a non stick small frying pan and add a teaspoon of cumin seeds to the heated pan. Stir with a wooden spoon for a few seconds, about 15-20 seconds and remove from heat. Continue stirring for even toasting until lightly toasted but not burnt. Transfer the toasted seeds into a bowl or a plate to stop the cooking process. Toasted seeds can be lightly ground using a mortar and pestle, grinding will enhance the flavor of the toasted cumin.

Raita is a popular addition to an Indian/ Pakistani meal.

- 2 cups yogurt
- ½ cup non fat milk (or ½ cup water)
- 3 tablespoons sugar
- ¼ teaspoon salt
- ½ teaspoon fresh ground black pepper
- ½ teaspoon toasted* cumin seeds
- ¼ teaspoon crushed red pepper (optional)
- 2 tablespoons chopped cilantro
- 2 tablespoons chopped green onions
- ½ cup chopped cucumber
- ½ cup julienned carrots
- 1 medium granny smith apple chopped
- 2 tablespoons toasted sesame seeds (optional)

In a mixing bowl blend the yogurt and milk until smooth. Add sugar, salt, ground black pepper and the crushed red pepper. Fold in the cilantro, green onions, cucumber, carrots, the chopped apple and the toasted sesame seeds.
Transfer to a serving bowl.
Chill before serving.
Garnish with chopped cilantro and ground cumin.

Fresh Ripe Mango Chutney With Lemon And Lime

Serves 8-12

Like the right accessories completing an outfit, made from ripe mangoes this chutney dresses up a meal in the same elegance. It's quick to fix yet will make you look like a pro and add flair to your table at the same time.

- 2 tablespoons butter
- 2 tablespoons fresh ginger root chopped
- 2 tablespoons cilantro finely chopped
- a pinch of salt
- 6 tablespoons sugar
- 2 tablespoons lemon juice
- 2 tablespoons lime juice
- ¾ cup of water
- ¼ teaspoon dry dill weed
- ¼ teaspoon cumin powder
- 1 teaspoon lemon and lime peel
- 4 medium size ripe mangoes peeled and diced
- 4 tablespoons sugar

Heat one tablespoon butter in a saucepan over medium heat and add the chopped ginger to the pan. Cook ginger in butter stirring occasionally, about 2 minutes until ginger is lightly glazed and begins to release flavor. Add cilantro and cook for another couple of minutes stirring constantly. Add salt and the 6 tablespoons of sugar. Cook for about half a minute and add the measured lemon and lime juices, cook for another 10 seconds, add water to the pan and let the mixture boil over medium low heat until the sugar dissolves and the mixture in the pan begins to thicken. Add half of the dry dill weed and half of the cumin powder. Cook the mixture for about 5 to 7 minutes or until the sauce thickens slightly. Remove from heat and let cool, add the lemon and lime peel.

In another saucepan heat one tablespoon of butter and add the remaining dill and the cumin powder to the butter and cook for about 20 seconds. Add the chopped mangoes to the saucepan folding until the mangoes heat through. Sprinkle 4 tablespoons of sugar over the warm mangoes and fold in. Add cooked mangoes to the cooling sauce and gently fold in. Refrigerate chutney and cool completely before serving. Mango chutney can be prepared up to two days ahead.

Serving Suggestions:

Serve as a condiment with barbecued meat, fried snacks and or vegetable samosas. It's great as a salad topping as well.

Baingan Raita

(Eggplant Raita)

In recipes that call for frying an eggplant, I am generally cautious on the frying part, especially in the use of the amount of oil. The eggplant is like a sponge and will soak up oil in a hurry. So for frying the vegetable, I warm up the oil for a few seconds and then brush the eggplant slices on both sides with the warm oil. Then layer the oil brushed slices in a heated non-stick frying pan and lightly fry on both sides. Fried slices can then be drained on a paper towel to remove any excess oil.

- ½ teaspoon cumin seeds lightly toasted and coarsely ground
- Salt to taste
- 2 cloves of garlic pureed
- ⅛ teaspoon dried dill weed
- 2 cups yogurt
- ¾ cup milk or water
- ⅛ teaspoon crushed red pepper
- one medium sized eggplant washed, dried and sliced in rounds (with the skin on)
- ¼ cup warm oil for brushing the eggplant slices

For Garnish:
- 2 tablespoons chopped cilantro
- 1 tablespoon of finely chopped green onion.

Mix the first seven ingredients in a bowl, cover and refrigerate.
(Can be prepared 6-8 hours ahead of serving time)

Warm oil in a bowl in the microwave or in a frying pan, for 30-45 seconds or a little more if needed, to where it is warmed up well, thinned out a little but definitely not smoking! With a pastry brush, brush the slices with the warm oil on both sides, using a quick stroke of the brush so as not to over oil the slices.

Fry the slices on both sides, lightly (2-3 minutes) and drain. Let cool to room temperature, add the fried slices to the yogurt mixture and fold in gently. Pour Raita into a serving bowl, garnish with chopped cilantro and the chopped green onion, and serve.

Kheera aur Bengan Raita

(Egg Plant and Cucumber Raita)

Serves 8-10

Lightly fried and then cooled eggplant slices and grated or julienned cucumbers blend in together then lightly seasoned for a cool condiment.

- 1 Japanese eggplant thin sliced (unpeeled)
- 4 tablespoons oil
- 1 teaspoon cumin seeds toasted*
- ¼ teaspoon cayenne Pepper
- ½ teaspoon fresh ground black pepper
- ½ teaspoon salt
- 2 tablespoons sugar
- ½ cup chopped green onions
- 4 tablespoons chopped cilantro
- 2 tablespoons lemon juice
- 1 cup grated cucumber
- 1 teaspoon dried dill weed (optional)
- 1 chopped tomato and a tablespoon of chopped cilantro for garnish

* see directions to toast cumin seeds under chapter on spices

Warm the oil for 15-20 seconds in the microwave using a glass or ceramic bowl.

With a pastry brush, brush both sides of the sliced eggplant with the warm oil.

Heat a non stick frying pan, arrange eggplant slices in the pan, layering if necessary. Sauté the slices uncovered for a couple of minutes turning over once or twice. Cover the pan, reduce heat and let them get tender in their own steam. Approximate cooking time is 5 minutes-cool completely. Add cumin seeds, cayenne pepper, black pepper, salt and sugar to the yogurt and mix well. Add the green onions, cilantro, lemon juice, dill weed, eggplant slices and the grated cucumber and mix well. Garnish with cilantro. Chill well before serving.

Serves 6-8

Cucumber Raita

Make sure to chill this raita well in the refrigerator before serving. It is a heavenly condiment for summer meals, but don't let anyone stop you from enjoying it during the winter months as well. The recipe below is a good basic recipe and it can certainly be modified to include additional vegetables of your choice.

Ingredients:

- 2 cups yogurt
- ½ cup milk
- ½ teaspoon toasted cumin seeds*
- ½ teaspoon or to taste fresh ground black pepper
- ½ teaspoon salt
- 1 teaspoon sugar
- 2 tablespoons finely chopped green onion
- 1 tablespoon chopped cilantro (stems and leaves together)
- ½ teaspoon dried dill weed
- 2 cucumbers peeled and finely chopped or julienned
- for garnish a pinch of dill weed and a tablespoon chopped cilantro

* see chapter on 'spices' for directions on toasting cumin seeds

Mix the yogurt and milk, then add the toasted cumin, salt, ground black pepper and sugar. Fold in the green onions, cilantro, dill weed and the cucumbers. Adjust the seasoning if needed to your palate, pour in a serving bowl, cover and store in the refrigerator until ready to serve. Garnish with some chopped cilantro and a pinch of dried dill weed and enjoy.

Serves 4-6

Vegetable Dishes
The Indian/Pakistani Way

Blended in herbs and spiced up for flavor these recipes favor any palate and equally please any age group.

The herbs and spices make them appetizing enough to please grown ups and kids alike. There is an old saying in India and Pakistan that goes, *"saag pakaay makhan ghee aur bari baho ka naam"*, literally: 'before you compliment the older daughter-in-law for the (well cooked) spinach, know that the real credit belongs to the *ghee* and butter'.

I would add that butter is not the only culprit here, the herbs and spices are equally to blame. I grew up loving vegetables in general, especially spinach; and that

being my favorite, then okra, potatoes and kachnar. *Kachnar,* is the bud of the orchid family of flowers, hits the market in Lahore, during early spring and is available for a short window of 3-4 weeks. The point is that the creative and clever use of spices and herbs in cooking vegetable dishes can make the veggies appetizing enough for even a growing child. In my recipes I use mostly olive or grape seed oil.

So, if you are looking for a successful solution to the challenge of making your kids eat vegetable you are holding the right book and are at the right chapter. Explore the possibilities, and have fun experimenting.

Aloo (Palak) Methi

(Spinach cooked with potatoes, seasoned with fenugreek (methi) leaves)

Aloo Methi is a mildly flavored vegetable side dish cooked in a base of sautéed onions, ginger and garlic and seasoned with mild spices and fresh herbs. It is a perfect side dish with grilled food. I can assure you this dish will make any child love spinach with or without *Popeye*.

- ¼ cup olive oil
- ½ teaspoon cumin seeds
- ¼ cup chopped cilantro
- 1 tablespoon chopped fresh ginger root
- 1 bunch green onions chopped (optional)
- 1 medium sized onion thin sliced or finely chopped

- 1 slightly heaping teaspoon pureed ginger
- 1 slightly heaping teaspoon pureed garlic
- 1 teaspoon salt
- ½ teaspoon crushed red pepper
- 1 teaspoon coriander powder
- ½ teaspoon turmeric powder
- 4 white potatoes cut in chunks
- 1 16 oz package chopped frozen spinach, (covered with a wet paper towel and micro waved for 5-6 minutes in a bowl with ¼ cup water)
- 1 tablespoon dried fenugreek leaves
  (AKA: Methi, available at Indian spice stores)
- 1 Serrano chili seeded and chopped
- Water as cooking aid

Directions:

Heat oil in a saucepan until hot but not smoking; add cumin seeds, one tablespoon of chopped cilantro, chopped ginger and chopped green onions, sauté herbs for a minute to help flavor the oil.

Add chopped brown onion and sauté for about 5-7 minutes, until most of the water from onions has evaporated and it starts to turn a light gold at the edges. (As oil in the pot begins to re-surface around the sautéed onions, you are ready to proceed to the next step) Add pureed ginger and garlic and stir often as you sauté the mix for a few seconds to a minute.

Add salt, crushed red pepper, ground coriander, turmeric and continue to sauté. Keep an eye on spice mixture as you sauté, add a few drops of water every couple of minutes to keep it from sticking to the bottom of the pan, and continue to sauté for 3-5 minutes.

Add potatoes and coat them well with the spices, cook uncovered for 3-5 minutes. Add 2-4 tablespoons of water cover the pot and let potatoes cook for 9-12 minutes on a low flame. Uncover the pan and stir; add the prepared spinach, fold it in the spice mixture with potatoes. Cover the pan and let cook for 15-20 minutes on a medium low flame. Check periodically and give it a stir to ensure even cooking and to keep the dish from sticking to the bottom of the pan.

Vegetables generally cook in their own liquid but add a few drops of water if needed or if the mix seems too dry. Inset the tip of a well pointed knife in a potato piece to check for doneness. The knife should insert with ease and the potato wedge must not offer resistance. Sprinkle with dried fenugreek leaves (Methi). Turn heat off, add the chopped Serrano chilies cover and let sit for a few minutes before serving.

Serving Suggestions: Serve with rice, chappatis (Indian flat bread) or pita bread
Serves 6-8

Store leftovers in the refrigerator in an air tight container for up to 2-4 days

Aloo Ghobi Mattar

(Potatoes cooked with Cauliflower and Peas)

I like this dish to have a bright yellow hue, so I use crushed red pepper instead of cayenne. That allows turmeric to dominate the color of the dish. Even though in this variation I use peas along with potatoes and cauliflower, the dish can be cooked with potatoes and cauliflower alone, omitting the peas altogether.

- ¼ cup cooking oil
- ¼ teaspoon cumin seeds
- 1 tablespoon julienned fresh ginger
- 2 Serrano chilies seeded, washed, thinly sliced or chopped
- 1 bunch green onion chopped
- 1 cup chopped cilantro
- 2 medium sized (yellow) onions chopped
- 1 slightly heaping teaspoon pureed ginger
- 1 slightly heaping teaspoon pureed garlic
- 1 teaspoon salt
- ½ teaspoon turmeric
- ½ teaspoon crushed red pepper
- ½ teaspoon ground cumin
- 1 teaspoon ground coriander
- 3 medium potatoes (Peel and cut potatoes into medium chunks—Soak pieces in cold water until ready to use)
- 3-4 cups cauliflower florets (cut the larger pieces into a smaller size)
- 2 cups frozen green peas
- Water as cooking aid

For garnish: cilantro and garam massala (optional)

Heat oil in a deep saucepan or frying pan; add the cumin seeds, julienned ginger, green chilies, scallions (green onions) and half of the cilantro. Cook for 2 to 3 minutes stirring well; add the chopped (yellow) onions and cook as you continue to stir until the onions are translucent, this should take between 10 to 15 minutes.

At this stage add the pureed ginger and garlic and sauté for a few seconds. Add the salt, turmeric, crushed red pepper, ground cumin and the ground coriander.

Sauté the spices for 5 to 7 minutes, stir to keep them from sticking to the bottom of the pan, reduce heat slightly if needed and add a tablespoon or two of water to the spice mixture as you continue to sauté.

Add the potatoes and cook for about 7-10 minutes, add the cauliflower* stir the vegetables coating them well with the spices and herbs in the pan.

Add the remaining cilantro, cook uncovered for about five minutes and then cover the pan and let the

*A short cut tip to prep cauliflower florets before adding them to the potatoes:
To speed up the cooking time for this dish, take the cauliflower florets and put them in a glass or ceramic bowl. Sprinkle with a couple of tablespoons of water, 2 tablespoons chopped cilantro, 1 tablespoon of chopped green onions, some salt and 1 tablespoon of cooking oil. Fold the cauliflower florets to coat well with these ingredients. Cover the bowl with a damp paper towel and microwave for 3 ½ minutes before adding them to the potatoes.

Caution:
If employing the above step, cover the pot and cook the potatoes for 3-5 minutes longer before adding the micro waved cauliflower florets to the pot. Fold the micro waved cauliflower florets in the spice mixture to coat well with the sautéed spices, finish cooking following the recipe above.

vegetables cook in their own steam for about 20 minutes, uncover and stir to check for doneness. Add the peas-cover and reduce heat if needed, cook for another 7 to 10 minutes. Uncover and cook on low heat partially covered to allow any excess water to evaporate.

Transfer to a serving dish, garnish with chopped cilantro and garam massala before serving.

Serves 6-8

Palak Paneer (or saag paneer)

(Spinach cooked with cheese)

Spinach and cheese (use Indian cheese, available at most Indian spice stores in the U.S.) cooked in an aromatic blend of herbs and mild spices. The cheese cubes are lightly fried first, drained on a paper towel and then added to the cooked spinach.

Restaurants often use cream for this recipe; my recipe here calls for yogurt as a healthier alternative.

To boil the spinach:
- 2, 16 oz. packages chopped frozen spinach
- 2 cups water
- 3-4 mashed cloves of garlic.
- Pinch of salt

For the Curry Base:
- ¼ cup olive oil or any cooking oil
- 2 " piece of ginger root julienned
- 1 bunch green onions chopped
- ¼ cup chopped cilantro
- 2 Serrano chilies seeded and chopped
- 1 ½ medium sized (yellow) onion chopped or thin sliced
- 2 heaping teaspoons pureed garlic
- 1 teaspoon salt

- ½ teaspoon cayenne pepper
- ½ teaspoon crushed red pepper
- ½ teaspoon cumin powder
- 1 teaspoon coriander powder
- ½ cup yogurt (blended smooth)

- 1 ½ cup cubed and fried homemade cheese (recipe follows) or 1 package *paneer* (Indian cheese available at most Indian spice stores) cubed and fried
- Water as cooking aid

For spinach prep:
Boil spinach in water, garlic cloves and salt for about 10 minutes and drain or micro wave for 5-7 minutes with ¼ cup of water in a glass bowl, cover the bowl with a moist paper towel to microwave.

For the base Curry:
Heat oil in a saucepan; add the ginger, green onion, cilantro, ½ of the green chilies and the chopped (yellow) onion. Stir often as you sauté to flavor the oil with the herbs. Cook until most of the water from the onion has evaporated and you begin see to the oil surface again in the pot-about 8-12 minutes. Add the pureed garlic and sauté for a few seconds.

A note of caution on frying cheese:

Indian cheese, homemade or store bought tends to hold some moisture and the oil may start to splatter as soon as the slices are added to the hot oil for frying. To minimize the splattering of oil, let the sliced cheese sit at room temperature in a plate for about 15-20 minutes, spread the pieces out in a single layer, this will allow for most of the moisture to evaporate and greatly reduce the splattering of oil.

Add the salt, cayenne pepper, the crushed red pepper, cumin powder and the coriander powder. Cook as you stir another 3 to 5 minutes on medium heat. Add yogurt, blend it smooth into the cooking herbs and spices.

Add the prepared spinach stir to fold the spinach in the spices, cover and cook on medium low heat for about 20 minutes. Transfer ⅓ of the spinach mixture to a food processor and puree for a few seconds with ½ or ¾ cup water, return the pureed spinach to the pot. Reduce heat, cover and let simmer for another 15 minutes, add the fried cheese cubes, fold them in the cooking spinach and continue to simmer for an additional 7 to 10 minutes. Keep covered until ready to serve.

Serve with basmati rice or naan, garnished with chopped cilantro and the remaining green chilies.

Homemade cheese:

- 1 gallon whole milk
- 3/4 cup lemon juice (fresh squeezed or bottled)
- oil for frying the cheese

Heat milk in a deep cooking pot. As the milk starts to boil add the lemon juice and stir. Continue to boil for 3-4 minutes; the acid will separate the milk, the solid curd will rise to the top separating from the whey below. Reduce heat and let the liquid simmer for 2-3 minutes, turn heat off and allow the pot to cool for 10-15 minutes.

Strain the whey in a strainer lined with a double layer of cheese cloth. Twist and tie the cheese cloth tightly, let the cheese drain completely, about 3 to 4 hours. Untie and wrap the formed cheese in plastic, refrigerate until ready to use (can be refrigerated for approx. 2 to 3 days). Cut in cubes, fry lightly to a soft golden color, drain on paper towels, and season warm cubes with salt. Fried cheese pieces can be frozen in a zip lock bag.

Serves 8

Aloo Gajjar Mattar

Potatoes, carrots and peas cooked in mild spices and herbs, with onions and tomatoes.

Serves 6-8

- ¼ cup olive oil or any other vegetable oil
- ¼ teaspoon cumin seeds
- 2 tablespoons julienned ginger
- ½ cup chopped cilantro
- 1 medium onion finely chopped
- 1 teaspoon pureed ginger
- 1 teaspoon pureed garlic
- 1 teaspoon salt or to taste
- ½ teaspoon crushed red pepper
- ¼ teaspoon ground red pepper
- ½ teaspoon ground cumin
- 1 teaspoon ground coriander
- 3 medium white potatoes cut in chunks
- 3 cups peeled and sliced carrots
- 2 medium tomatoes seeded and chopped
- 1 cup frozen peas
- 1 Serrano chili thin sliced (optional)
- one pinch of garam massala for garnish
- Water as cooking aid

Heat oil in a pot or a deep frying pan; add the cumin seeds, julienned ginger, a couple of tablespoons of the chopped cilantro and sauté on medium flame for a few seconds. Add the chopped onion, another tablespoon of the chopped cilantro and cook on a medium flame until most of the water from the onion has evaporated and it begins to have a glazed/glossy appearance and starts to turn a light golden color at the edges, about 8-10 minutes.

Add the pureed ginger and garlic to the sautéed onion stir and cook for a couple of minutes then add the salt, crushed red pepper, ground red pepper, ground cumin and coriander. Sauté the spices for 3-5 minutes. Add a few drops of water if needed to keep the spice mixture from over drying.

Add the potato chunks and fold them into the spice mixture, cook for a 5-6 minutes. Add the sliced carrots, the chopped tomatoes and cook uncovered for three to four minutes, then cover the pot, reduce the flame and let the vegetables cook for about 10 to 15 minutes. Check the contents in the pot every few minutes; stir the vegetables for even cooking, and also to avoid them from sticking to the bottom of the pan or an accidental charring. If needed add a few drops of water to keep contents moist.

Check for doneness by inserting the tip of a sharp knife in one of the potato pieces, the knife should insert through the potato with ease. Cover and continue cooking if needed for another few minutes until the vegetables are tender. Add the peas towards the end and steam the vegetables together for another couple of minutes. Turn off the flame and let the dish rest in a covered pot for about five minutes before serving. Garnish with chopped cilantro, the sliced Serrano chili and a pinch of garam massala if desired.

Mattar Paneer

Peas cooked in a creamy yogurt sauce with cheese.

Indian and Pakistani markets and grocery stores now carry paneer or the Indian cheese commercially made in their refrigerator sections; it is available packaged and labeled 'paneer'.

To Fry Cheese:

Slice the cheese in desired size pieces, heat oil in a small frying pan and gently add the cheese pieces. Lightly fry one side for a few minutes until a light gold brown color then flip the sides. Drain on a plate lined with paper towels.

A Note to Frying Cheese: When frying cheese use the following steps and precautions.

Indian cheese, homemade or store bought tends to hold moisture and when moist cheese is added to the hot oil, the oil may start to splatter. To avoid the oil from splashing, air dry sliced cheese, spread the sliced cheese pieces out in a single layer on a plate and let sit for 10-15 minutes. This will allow for most of the moisture to evaporate and minimize oil splatter.

For the Curry Sauce

- ¼ cup oil
- 1 medium onion sliced thin
- a pinch of cumin seeds
- 1 black/brown cardamom
- 1 tablespoon julienned ginger
- ½ cup chopped cilantro
- 1 heaping teaspoon pureed ginger
- ½ teaspoon paprika
- ¼ teaspoon cayenne pepper
- ½ teaspoon ground coriander
- 1 teaspoon salt
- 2 tablespoons full cream yogurt
- 6 medium tomatoes chopped
- Water as a cooking aid

- 1 Package Indian cheese bought at the Indian food store (cut up into small squares or cubes) or
- 1 ½ cups thick sliced homemade Indian cheese (See homemade Indian cheese recipe under: *Shared steps and techniques . . .)* at the end of the book, p. 215
- 8 oz frozen peas
- Oil for frying cheese squares

For the Curry Sauce

Heat oil in a sauce pan over a medium flame, sauté onions with the cumin seeds and the black cardamom; add 2 tablespoons of chopped cilantro and the julienned ginger as the onions are cooking to flavor the oil. Sauté until the onions are a light golden brown, stir as you sauté. About 8-12 minutes.

Add the pureed ginger, cook for a couple of minutes stirring for even cooking of the herb and onion mix. As the ginger lends it's aroma to the dish add the paprika, cayenne pepper, ground coriander and salt. Sauté the spices for a good 10-15 minutes, adding a few drops of water every 2-3 minutes to keep the mix from over drying or browning and sticking to the bottom of the pan.

Add the yogurt to the spice mixture and blend well. Cook for 3-5 minutes. Now add the chopped tomatoes and continue cooking for another ten minutes. At this point, transfer ¾ of the pot's contents into a food processor and process until smooth. This is done to cut down on the cooking time as well as smooth out the curry. Transfer the pureed contents back into the cooking pot; add ½ a cup of water to the processor to empty out the processor container completely.

Simmer on low heat for about 10 minutes; add the fried cheese cubes and the peas. Cover and continue to simmer for another 10-15 minutes. Turn off the heat and let the dish rest for a few minutes before serving.
Garnish with a few hard boiled eggs and cilantro if desired.

Serve with rice or naan bread
Serves 6-8

Massala Bengan

(Eggplant cooked in a tomato based curry sauce)

This recipe is a fun way to enjoy eggplant. It is sure to shift the palate paradigm of the toughest 'vegetable' sell in the family. Eggplants do soak up oil like a sponge, so I brush them lightly with warm oil and then place them in a heated frying pan in a single layer to sauté. They will have the fried taste and yet not totally drenched in oil.

Ingredients

- ½ cup olive oil or any cooking oil of your preference
- 2 tablespoons chopped cilantro
- ½ bunch green onions chopped
- ½ teaspoon cumin seeds
- 2 medium size onions thin sliced
- 2 teaspoons (slightly heaping) garlic pureed
- salt to taste

- 1 teaspoon crushed red pepper
- ½ teaspoon ground red pepper
- 1 teaspoon ground coriander
- ¼ teaspoon turmeric powder
- ½ teaspoon ground cumin
- 8-10 medium tomatoes seeded and chopped
- 3-4 medium sized Japanese eggplants, washed and sliced (with skin on)
- ½ cup yogurt blended smooth
- some water as cooking aid

Directions:

Heat oil in a deep pot over a medium flame; add cilantro, chopped green onions and cumin seeds. Next add the sliced onions and sauté until all

50

the water from the onions has evaporated, stir often as you sauté for even cooking, about 10-15 minutes.

When the onions begin to appear translucent and start to turn a light golden brown at the edges, add the pureed garlic, stir for a few seconds until the garlic begins to lend it's aroma to the pot and is sautéed slightly.

Add the spices, the salt, crushed and ground red pepper, ground coriander, turmeric and the ground cumin. Sauté the spices for 5-7 minutes, stir as you sauté the spices to keep them from sticking to the bottom of the pan. If the spices seem to dry up too much add a few drops of water every couple of minutes to cool down the onion and spice mixture and to keep it from over browning or burning.

Add chopped tomatoes; cook about 5 minutes with the pot uncovered. Cover the pot and continue cooking for another 10-15 minutes. Reduce heat add ½ cup of water and let simmer for 10-15 minutes longer to form a nice rich curry sauce-stir often as you simmer; if the sauce seems too dry add a few drops of water as it cooks and lower heat.

Slice eggplant (un-peeled) in round slices. In a separate deep pan heat up some oil, brush both sides of eggplant slices quickly with warm oil. Sauté the oil brushed eggplant slices cooking lightly on each side until tender, drain on a paper towel.

Add fried eggplant gently to the simmering sauce, cover and let cook for another five minutes. Pour contents into a serving dish, top with blended yogurt and garnish with some chopped cilantro. Massala bengan is great with rice and/or chappatis.

Serves 6-8

Bengan Bharta

(Smoked and pureed eggplant cooked in a blend of onion, tomatoes and herbs)

This is one of my favorite ways to cook eggplant. This recipe has a couple of labor intensive steps, but totally worth it. The curry sauce for cooking eggplant must be heavy in tomatoes, a tip I picked up from my family's kitchen growing up. The eggplant needs that tartness of tomatoes for a richer and a more flavorful taste

- 1 large eggplant
- ½ teaspoon oil to rub the eggplant skin
- 6 tablespoons cooking oil
- ¼ teaspoon cumin seeds
- 1 large onion sliced
- 1 cup chopped cilantro
- 7 -10 cloves of garlic pureed
- 1 teaspoon salt
- ½ teaspoon ground red pepper (cayenne)
- 6-8 medium tomatoes chopped
- 2 Serrano green chilies
- water as cooking aid

Grilling and smoking the eggplant:
Rub the eggplant skin lightly with oil, place it directly over an open flame from your stove or outside on the grill and roast. Turn frequently until the skin is charred on all sides and the eggplant is soft.

Once it is done on all sides put it inside a paper bag and set it aside, about 7-10 minutes or until cooled enough to handle.

For the curry sauce:
Heat oil in a deep pan on a medium flame, add cumin seeds, sliced onions and 2 tablespoons of chopped cilantro; sauté the sliced onions until most of the water from the onions has evaporated and they begin to turn a light

golden brown around the edges, about 10-15 minutes. This is an approximate time it would take for the onions to lightly brown; keep stirring and watch closely as you sauté.

At this point add the pureed garlic and cook for a minute. Add the salt and the ground red pepper. Cook these spices for about 7-10 minutes, stirring frequently and adding a few drops of water if the mixture dries up too much, add the chopped tomatoes. Let the spice and tomato mixture cook for about 10-12 minutes.

Transfer half of the tomato and spice mixture into the container of a blender or food processor and puree. Pour back into the pot, using a cup of water to completely empty the blender bowl, cover and let the sauce simmer on a low flame for 25 to 30 minutes.

While the spice and tomato mixture is cooking peel the roasted eggplant, remove and discard the stem. Chop the eggplant and puree in a food processor. Add the pureed eggplant to the pot. Again, if needed use a little water to fully empty the contents of the blender.

Partially uncover the pot and continue cooking for another 10-15 minutes. The dish is done when most for the water from the vegetables has evaporated and some of the oil has begun to surface on the sides. Add the whole green chilies and cover the pot until ready to serve.

Garnish with cilantro.
Serve with plain boiled rice and or chappatis.

Serves 4-6

Kalonji Aloo

(Potatoes cooked with Nigella seeds)

Kalonji Aloo is a quick to make side dish with minimal ingredients. Yet it comes out delicious and appealing. It is a good side addition any main course.

- 5 tablespoon cooking oil
- 4-5 medium tomatoes chopped
- 1 teaspoon salt
- ½ teaspoon ground red pepper
- 4-5 med potatoes peeled, cut lengthwise into thick wedges and set in a bowl of water until ready to use
- ½ teaspoon kalonji (available at Indian/Pakistani food stores)
- 2 Serrano green chilies, seeded chopped and cleaned
- ½ cup chopped cilantro
- some water as cooking aid

Heat oil in a cooking pan over a medium flame, add the chopped tomatoes and cook for about 10 minutes until the tomatoes begin to break and dissolve in the pan, add the salt and pepper. Continue to cook to for another minute or two.

Add the sliced potatoes cover and let simmer on medium low heat until the potatoes are tender. Insert the tip of a sharp knife in a potato wedge, knife should slide through with ease and the potato should not offer resistance. Time will vary between 15-20 minutes approximately. Maintain and adjust the amount of sauce around the vegetables by adding water, a couple of tablespoons at a time if needed.

Add the kalonji, green chili and a couple of tablespoons of the chopped cilantro. Cover and simmer for another 5-7 minutes, stir and add the remaining cilantro and serve.

Serves 4-6

Bhindi Kee Bhujia

Okra cooked in herbs and spices

In the right hands, with the right blend of herbs and spices and most of all with the right recipe okra _rules_; whether it's cooked by itself, in combination with another vegetable or my favorite, with moist, thick and juicy lamb chops, okra is delicious. Sometimes it will test your patience, at times it can be a little temperamental but don't let this veggie get away with it-maintain your confidence and control and I promise you _the vegetable_ will behave.

- ¼ of a cup olive oil
- ¼ teaspoon cumin seeds
- ¼ cup julienned ginger
- 4 tablespoons chopped cilantro
- 1 large onion chopped
- 1 heaping teaspoon pureed ginger
- 1 heaping teaspoon pureed garlic
- 1 teaspoon salt
- ¼ teaspoon ground cayenne pepper
- ½ teaspoon crushed red pepper
- ½ teaspoon ground cumin powder
- ½ teaspoon ground coriander powder
- 4 medium sized tomatoes seeded and chopped

To stir fry okra:
- 1 lb fresh okra,
- (washed, dried, stems removed and larger pieces cut in two)
- 2 tablespoons of oil to stir fry okra
- 1 teaspoon pureed ginger and garlic
- ½ teaspoon salt

Wash okra and drain completely. Then spread it on a paper towel and let dry. Remove the outer extended edge of the stem bit at the end (keeping the capped portion intact) and cut the large pieces into two, leave baby size okra whole.

Heat oil in an open frying pan, when sizzling hot add okra with the pureed ginger/garlic and salt, and give it a quick stir fry for 3-5 minutes.

The base sauce

Heat oil in a deep pan, add the cumin seeds, julienned ginger and the chopped cilantro. Let sizzle in warmed oil for 10-15 seconds and add the chopped onions. Sauté the onions on a medium flame for 10-12 minutes, stir often for even cooking.

When most of the water from the onions has evaporated and they start to look glazed, add the pureed ginger and garlic, stir and cook for about 20-30 seconds; add the salt and the cayenne pepper, crushed red pepper, ground cumin and coriander and stir and sauté for 3-4 minutes.

Combining stir fried okra and the base sauce

Add the prepared okra to the cooking spice and onion mixture in the pan, cook for about 8-10 minutes. Add the chopped tomatoes; cook uncovered on a medium flame for 6-8 minutes. Cover and simmer on a low flame for another 10-12 minutes until the okra is tender and cooked thru. Turn heat off, partially uncover the pot and let it rest for a few minutes before serving. Cooked okra should hold its shape and be tender at the same time. Simmer a few minutes longer if needed, based on the intensity of the flame and the thickness of the pot.

Serves 4-6

Aloo Bhindi

(Potatoes and Okra cooked in herbs and spices)

I never realized what a happy marriage these two vegetables create, how well they belong with each other until my sister-in-law Neelo shared this recipe with me. It starts with onions, like most Indian/Pakistani curries, ginger, garlic and then some of those magical spices and you have a heavenly treat. It is a perfect side dish and is great with rice or bread.

Aloo Bhindi Okra and Potato Cooked in Tomatoes and Herbs

- 4 tablespoons olive or grape seed oil
- 1/8 teaspoon cumin seeds
- 2 tablespoons julienned ginger
- 2 tablespoons chopped cilantro
- 1 medium onion chopped
- 1 heaping teaspoon pureed ginger
- 1 heaping teaspoon pureed garlic
- 1 teaspoon salt
- ½ teaspoon cayenne pepper
- ¼ teaspoon crushed red pepper

- 8-10 baby potatoes or
- 3 medium white potatoes cut in desired size chunks
- 3 medium tomatoes seeded and chopped
- 1/8 teaspoon dried dill weed

To sauté okra:

- 1-1½ lbs fresh okra
- 1 tablespoon oil
- 1 tablespoon julienned ginger
- ½ teaspoon pureed ginger
- ½ teaspoon pureed garlic

- 1/8 teaspoon crushed red pepper
- ¼ teaspoon salt

Wash okra and drain completely. Then spread on a paper towel and let dry. Remove the stem bit at the end and cut the large pieces into two, leave any baby size okra as is. Wash the potatoes and cut them in desired size chunks and set aside until ready to use. If I am using the yellow Yukon gold potatoes, I wash them well and usually leave them unpeeled.

Heat oil in a deep pan and add the cumin seeds, julienned ginger and the chopped cilantro. Let sizzle in warmed oil for 10-15 seconds and add the chopped onion. Sauté the onions on medium heat for 10-12 minutes and stir for even cooking.

When most of the water from the onion has evaporated and the onion starts to turn translucent and a light golden color at the edges, add the pureed ginger and garlic, stir and cook for about 20-30 seconds. Add the salt, cayenne pepper and the crushed red pepper, stir often and sauté for 3-4 minutes. Now add the chunked potatoes and cook uncovered for about 10 minutes, stir in the chopped tomatoes, cover and cook on medium low heat for roughly 15 minutes.

To sauté the okra:

As the potatoes are cooking, in another pot heat the 1 tablespoon oil, add the cut okra, ginger garlic puree, the julienned ginger, crushed red pepper and sprinkle with salt. Sauté on medium high flame and stir often as you sauté. Cook for about 10-12 minutes.

Add the sautéed okra to the potato mix. If the base sauce in the potato mix is too dry add ¼ of a cup of water to the pot. Cover and simmer on a medium low flame for about another 10-15 minutes until the potatoes are done. Test the potatoes for doneness by inserting a sharp knife into a potato wedge.

Enjoy with rice, chappatis or naan.

Serves 4-6

Sarsoon Ka Saag

(Mustard greens cooked in onions and mild herbs)

Sarsoon ka saag, or mustard greens is a very popular Punjabi dish typically savored with 'corn bread' (tortilla style) coated with warm melted butter-umm umm umm . . . and like lentils (daals) it is topped with a topping of sautéed onions and ginger as the final step before serving. Popular during the winter months, the natural season for mustard greens.

For the Saag:
4 cups water
2 16 oz packets frozen chopped mustard greens
1 16 oz package frozen chopped spinach
1 green chili, pureed in the processor (with seeds)
Salt to taste
½ cup whole wheat flour
¼ stick butter

For the Bhigar or grilled onion topping:
- ½ teaspoon crushed red pepper or 4 whole dried red chili peppers
- 1 onion peeled and thin sliced
- 2 Serrano chilies seeded and thin sliced

- 2 tablespoons peeled and julienned ginger
- 2 cloves of garlic slightly pounded
- 1/3 cup oil

In a deep pot add the water, mustard greens, spinach, the green chili and salt. Cover, and let the greens cook in boiling water until most of the water has evaporated but not totally dried, about 40 minutes. At this stage sprinkle the flour over the cooked greens and mix well with a wooden spoon or a potato masher so the flour is incorporated well without forming any lumps.

Pour half of the cooked greens in a food processor and give it a quick pulsing action, not to process it completely but just pureeing it slightly. Pour it back in the pot with the rest of the cooked dish and continue to simmer and stir over a low flame for 25-30 minutes, stir in butter.

For the Bhigar or grilled onion topping:
You can start preparing onion topping as the greens simmer.

Heat oil in a deep frying pan; add the sliced onions and let cook until they begin to turn a light golden brown. Fry them on a medium flame for even browning. Add the crushed red pepper, ginger and garlic. Cook for another few minutes until the ginger and garlic begin to lend aroma to the pan. 30-45 seconds. Pour all of the mix over the cooked greens and serve with warmed naan, chappatis or tortillas. Preferably heated and lightly buttered corn tortillas. Garnish with sliced Serrano chilies.

Garnish with Serrano chilis.
Serves 8-10

Malai Kofta

Vegetable 'meatballs' in a Creamy Curry Sauce

Serves 6-8

Koftas are typically made with ground meat, that's what the term kofta usually refers to, a meatball. Here the term is borrowed and applied to a vegetarian's version of a meatball. A clever mix of nuts and vegetables are used here to mimic a regular meat kofta and served in a tomato based curry sauce.

- 2 cups finely pureed cauliflower
- 1 cup finely pureed carrots
- 1 cup pureed 'Indian cheese' (*paneer*) (homemade or store bought)*
- 1 teaspoon cumin powder
- ¼ teaspoon Garam Massala
- ½ cup finely chopped green onion
- 2 tablespoons finely chopped cilantro
- ½ cup coarsely chopped raw cashews
- ¼ cup raisins
- 1 teaspoon salt
- 6 table spoons gram flour
- Vegetable Oil for frying

*For Directions on making homemade cheese please refer to the chapter on:
'Shared Steps, Ingredients and Methods' at the end of the book, page 215

Mix well all of the above ingredients in a bowl and form (reasonably tight) patties resembling oval meatballs. Using approximately 2 tablespoons of the mix for each patty. Fry them gently and lightly on all sides in a thin layer of vegetable oil heated to about 350°. Drain on paper towels and set aside.

For The Curry Sauce:
- ¼ cup oil
- ¼ teaspoon cumin seeds

- ½ onion finely chopped
- 2 tablespoons finely chopped cilantro
- 1 heaping teaspoon pureed garlic (6-8 cloves)
- ½ teaspoon cumin powder
- ½ teaspoon cayenne pepper
- ½ teaspoon paprika
- 1 teaspoon salt
- 6-8 medium tomatoes pureed
- ¼ cup tomato sauce
- 6 tablespoons heavy cream or well blended full cream yogurt
- Water as cooking aid

For the Sauce:

Heat oil in a cooking pot over medium flame and add the cumin seeds, in another fifteen seconds add the onions and the cilantro. When the onions start to brown lightly, in about 5 to 7 minutes add the pureed garlic and cook for about 30 seconds, stirring as you cook to keep the garlic from browning.

At this point add the dry spices, the ground cumin, cayenne pepper, paprika and salt. Cook the spices for 7-10 minutes, for the flavors to blend in and to take the raw edge off the spices. Add a few drops of water to the pot every few minutes as you sauté the spices to keep the spice mixture from over browning or burning. This sautéing of spices is a very essential step in almost all curry dishes, and defines the quality of the final outcome of the dish.

Add the tomatoes and the tomato sauce, cover and cook the spice mixture on low heat. Cook for about 15-30 minutes till the mixture thickens a little. To help smooth the curry sauce puree ½ of the sauce mixture in a food processor or a blender and pour it back in the pot.

Add the cream, simmer until done. This may vary in time from 15 to 25 minutes. If the sauce seems too thick it can be diluted by adding a small amount of water, a couple of tablespoons at a time. Partially cover and let sit for a few minutes. Pour sauce in a serving dish and top with the drained fried vegetable koftas. Garnish with cilantro and enjoy.

Serves 6-8

Paneer Anday

(Sautéed Cheese Curry with Boiled Eggs)

Here is a very exclusive family recipe that has been enjoyed for generations within my immediate and extended family, and has passed the taste test equally with each generation. *'When I see paneer anday on the menu, I do not touch any other dish!'* was my niece's comment about this dish at a family dinner. And my daughter Naureen, in sharing her fond memories of how my mother always made sure to fix her favorite _dish_ when she went visiting grandma in Lahore, was making a reference to paneer anday as well. I know these girls are not expressing their sentiment alone, as this dish does get majority of the family's vote.

- ¼ cup oil

- 1 medium onion sliced thin
- a pinch of cumin seed
- 1 black/brown cardamom
- ½ cup chopped cilantro
- 2 teaspoons julienned ginger

- 1 heaping teaspoon pureed ginger
- 1 teaspoon salt

- ½ teaspoon paprika
- ¼ teaspoon cayenne pepper
- ½ teaspoon ground coriander (optional)
- 6-7 medium tomatoes (Roma tomatoes) seeded and chopped

- One 16-oz packet store bought Indian cheese (*paneer*) or homemade cheese (recipe on p. 215) sliced in approximate 1" to 1 ½" squares (about ¼" thick) and fried to a light golden color
- 6-8 eggs boiled and peeled

- oil for frying
- Water as cooking aid

Heat oil in a sauce pan; add sliced onions, cumin seeds and the black cardamom. Sauté on a medium flame, add 2 tablespoons of chopped cilantro and julienned ginger to flavor the oil as you sauté the onions.

Sauté until most of the water from the onions has evaporated and the oil begins to re-surface around the glazed onions. The onions will start to turn a light golden brown at the edges. Add the pureed ginger and cook for a couple of minutes, stir often as you sauté the ginger with the onions.

At this stage add the spices, the salt, paprika, cayenne pepper and the ground coriander and cook the spices for a good 10-15 minutes, adding a few drops of water every few minutes, as needed, to keep the contents from over browning or sticking to the bottom of the pan. The aim here is to braise/ sauté the spice mixture to remove the raw edge from the spices, at the same time making sure the mixture does not over cook.

Add the chopped tomatoes, cook for 8-10 minutes until tomatoes begin to dissolve in the pot. Puree half of the contents of the pot in a food processor or blender, and pour back into the pot to continue cooking. Add a cup of water to the processor or the blender to completely empty the remaining sauce bits and pour back in the pot

Pureeing the mixture helps cut down on the cooking time and smooth the sauce. Simmer on medium low heat for 20-25 minutes; in the meantime slice the cheese and sauté in hot oil for a few minutes on each side to a light golden brown and drain in a plate lined with a paper towel. Boil and peel eggs and set aside.

To Finish:

Once the sauce has cooked, and has reduced down to about ½ of the original amount, and the oil begins to surface around the edges of the sauce, add the fried cheese slices. Fold the cheese slices gently into the sauce. Partially cover the pot and let simmer another 5-7 minutes, stirring occasionally.

Just before serving add the peeled boiled eggs and fold them into the curry sauce, transfer to a serving bowl. Garnish with chopped cilantro before serving.

Serve with chappatis or parathas.
Serves 8-10

Mango Salad with almonds

Some of the best mango varieties in the world are grown in Pakistan and India. I have seen some superior mango varieties from Pakistan selling in many countries around the world and at many prominent retail establishments including *Harrods* in London. That is probably the reason I feel an 'emotional monopoly' on recipes with mangoes or let me put it this way. I personally feel a responsibility for creating more recipes using mangoes and that is exactly what I have done in the following salad recipe and even pleasantly surprised myself with the results.

- 1 large packet baby spinach salad pack
- 1 large mango peeled and diced
- 1small can mandarin oranges
- ¼ cup sliced almonds
- 1 cucumber peeled and diced or sliced
- 2 bananas thick sliced and quickly given a *lemon water bath and drained
- (For lemon water: add 3 to 4 tablespoons of lemon juice, any bottled variety from concentrate is fine or fresh if available, to a cup of chilled water)`
- 4 tablespoons chopped cilantro

In a large bowl fold together the spinach, oranges, mangoes, cucumber, bananas and the sliced almonds.

Dressing:
- ¼ cup lemon juice (fresh or bottled)
- ¼ cup olive oil or any vegetable oil
- a dash of hot sauce
- 2 tablespoons sugar
- ¼ teaspoon salt
- ¼ teaspoon ground black pepper

For the dressing:

Mix all of the ingredients for the dressing in a mixing bowl, blend them well using a spoon and set aside until ready to use. Fold in the dressing garnish with cilantro and serve.

Serves 4-6

Tandoori Chicken Salad

(With a grilled vegetable topping)

Whenever possible prepare your lettuce a few hours before serving. The lettuce will be firm and crisp, and makes for an appetizing salad.

Lettuce Prep:
Separate lettuce leaves, rinse them in cold water, and drain. Now put them in a plastic or a glass bowl. If placing in a glass bowl cover the bowl and refrigerate for one to two hours before serving. The lettuce will be crisp and full of life.

- 2 Tandoori chicken breasts grilled, use recipe on page: 111 or page 114
- ¾ of the head of lettuce or 16 oz mixed salad greens
- 1 cup chopped or julienned carrots
- 1 cup julienned cucumber (if possible use Persian cucumbers)
- 1 cup julienned or chunked apple (granny smith or gala)
- 1 tomato chopped

Grilled vegetable topping:
- 2 tablespoons chopped cilantro
- ½ cup diced red, green and yellow bell peppers
- ¼ medium onion chopped
- 1 tablespoon chopped or julienned ginger root
- 2 tablespoons oil
- ½ cup raita dressing, see page 26
- 4 tablespoons toasted pine nuts as garnish (optional)

Tear the prepared lettuce (see lettuce prep at the top) in desired size pieces and add all of the chopped and julienned vegetables. Cut the grilled chicken into thin strips and set aside.

For the grilled vegetable topping heat oil in a frying pan or skillet and add the ginger, onions, chopped cilantro and sauté for 2 minutes. Now add the chunked bell peppers, continuing to sauté on high heat for another 2-3 minutes, fold in the sliced chicken and remove from heat. Top the lettuce mix with the chicken and grilled vegetable toppings,

garnish with nuts and cilantro and serve.

Serve the raita dressing on the side.

Serves 6-8

Lentils

(Daals)

A dish of lentils is usually added as a side dish with a meal. There are many varieties of lentils used in Indian cooking, and just as many variations in cooking lentils. They can be cooked alone, with meat and often I cook two or three varieties together. It is a favorite side item for Indian/Pakistani meals. Lentils are typically served with a sautéed onion and herb topping for some added deliciousness and as a garnish.

In the Indian/Pakistani cooking their use extends to many other creative forms. For example, in the ground form they are used to make dumplings, as a binding agent for some variations of pan fried kabobs and the list goes on.

I am including just a couple of recipes here that again are quick to fix and will help as a nice addition to your menu. It is a great choice as a source of protein if you yourself are vegan or are entertaining friends that are.

Daals or lentils are available: whole (and unpeeled), split and split & peeled (husked). Most of the recipes I have included in this book call for 'split & peeled' daal (or lentils). If needed, most Indian & Pakistani spice stores will be happy to assist you with questions regarding identifying different varieties.

Bhunee Urad

(AKA: Maash) Daal

I remember growing up, this dish was typically served as a side dish for our family meals. Usually served for the afternoon meals. Fresh cut lemon wedges normally accompanied this daal, so you could add a little twist of lemon to your serving.

- ¼ cup oil
- a pinch of cumin seeds
- one black cardamom
- 2 onions sliced
- 2 tablespoons julienned ginger
- 4 tablespoons chopped cilantro
- 1 teaspoon pureed ginger
- 1 teaspoon pureed garlic
- 1 teaspoon salt
- ½ teaspoon cumin powder
- ½ teaspoon ground turmeric
- ½ teaspoon crushed red pepper
- 1 ½ cups *split and peeld Urad (Maash) daal (soak for about half an hour in 3-4 cups of water)
- 2 ½ cups water

To Serve:
- lemon wedges
- 1 tablespoon chopped cilantro
- 2 Serrano chilies seeded and chopped
- 1 tablespoon julienned ginger

Heat oil in a pan over medium flame; add the cumin seeds and the black cardamom, sauté for about 10 seconds. Next add the sliced onions, the julienned ginger and the chopped cilantro. Sauté the onions until most of the water from the onions has evaporated and they start to turn a light golden hue. Stir the onions often as you sauté them for an even light golden color. Add the pureed ginger and garlic. Stir to sauté these ingredients slightly just for a few seconds. Next add the salt, ground cumin, turmeric and the crushed red pepper. Sauté the spices for 3-4 minutes, stirring to avoid the spices from sticking to the bottom of the pan or burning, add a few drops of water every couple of minutes or so if the spices start to dry up as you are sautéing the spice mix. This step in the preparation of stove top Indian/Pakistani curries requires careful attention. Drain the soaked lentils in a colander, add the lentils to the spice mixture, and cook for a minute stirring to fold into the onion and spice mixture. Add water, cover and let cook on a medium flame. Lentils should be done in 30-40 minutes. Feel a few pieces between your thumb and forefinger to test for doneness. Lentil should be tender and break easily. If needed add some more water and cook a few minutes longer, you can also let simmer using a simmer plate. (10-15 minutes)

Cooking Option 2:
Cook on a medium or low flame on your stove top for the first 25-30 minutes, then finish by transferring the covered pot for steaming in a 250° oven for another 20-25 minutes. Again adding more water if needed.

Garnish with the chopped chili and cilantro. Serve with lemon wedges and julienned ginger on the side.

Serves 8-10

* When buying daal (lentils) from an Indian or Pakistani food market let the store know you are looking for split and peeled lentils or daal

Channay (AKA: Chollay)

(Garbanzo beans cooked in a curry base):

This dish plays many roles-the recipe stays the same but its use will depend on the time of day and sometimes on the day of the week. On a Sunday late morning with pooris or a paratha it is a perfect brunch item, in the afternoon with a cup of tea it is a perfect afternoon snack and then I see some Indian snack shops serve it as a topping to your samosa order if you should so prefer. And all that is on top of 'channas' being a popular side dish at parties.

- 2 cups dry chickpeas (garbanzo beans)
- (Soaked for 4-6 hours or over night in 1 teaspoon baking soda and enough boiling water so it rises about four inches above the surface of chickpeas) or
- 3 16 oz cans of chick peas, drained and rinsed
- 1 medium onion chopped finely in a food processor
- 1" piece of ginger chopped finely in a food processor
- 10 cloves of garlic chopped finely in a food processor
- 1 cup chopped cilantro
- 2 Serrano chilies seeded, washed and chopped
- ½ teaspoon ground red pepper (cayenne)
- ¼ cup oil
- Salt to taste
- 2 medium tomatoes chopped or chunked
- 1 teaspoon garam massala

Toasted Cumin and crushed red pepper mix:

- 1 teaspoon cumin and

- 1/2 teaspoon crushed red pepper (or one whole dry red pepper)
- Toast the crushed red pepper and the cumin seeds lightly in a hot pan and grind together. The fumes from the toasted pepper can be strong. Use care as you handle and keep away from your face.

Water for cooking chick peas

Heat oil in a cooking pot over medium heat and add the onions. Cook for a couple of minutes and add 2 tablespoons of the chopped cilantro. Cook and stir until the water from the onions starts to dry a little about 8-10 minutes. Add the ginger and garlic and continue to cook for 4-5 minutes, stirring to avoid ginger and garlic from over browning or burning. Add the red chili, salt and ¼ teaspoon of the cumin red pepper mix.

Cook the spices for about 15 minutes adding a few drops of water every 3-4 minutes or as they start to appear dry to avoid them from burning.

Drain the chick peas and rinse them with cold water, add them to the cooking pot. Add the tomatoes, garam massala and about 4 cups of water, cover and let cook on medium heat for about 30-40 minutes. As the chick peas are cooking, check them a couple of times during cooking to adjust the flame and the amount of water in the pot. Check the beans for doneness and add more water if needed. If the flame is too strong and is drying up the water too fast, lower the flame. Chick peas are done when tender. Hold one between finger and thumb, press to check for doneness. A well done bean will mash readily and still hold its shape in the pot.

Serve with an assortment of bread pieces including, pita, naan, pooris and paratha bites.

Garnish with cilantro, chopped tomatoes and sprinkle with the remaining ground toasted cumin and red pepper mix or garam massala.

Serves 8-10

Daal: (Lentils)

High in protein, daal is typically a favorite side dish with a main meal; at least it was in our home when I was growing up. The 'accidental' absence of this side dish would get my dad's attention in a heartbeat!

Lentils are generally cooked alone; however they can also be cooked with meat. An excellent binding agent, daals are added to some kebob and kofta dishes to hold the meat and vegetables together. Daals are a main ingredient in the preparation of many snacks and in the Indo/Pak region they also have had a reputation for being a 'poor man's' source of protein.

I like to mix two or three varieties and usually have been very successful with the results.

You may cook a single variety, and the rest of the ingredients will remain the same. Sometimes I even throw in a lamb or chicken meat piece with bone into the cooking pot, which lends added flavor to the dish. Or substitute homemade chicken stock (p.215) for water.

- 1 cup channa daal*
- ½ cup masoor daal (split and peeled)*
- ½ cup moong daal (split and peeled)*
- 1 medium onion or one bunch of green onions chopped
- 2 teaspoons pureed ginger
- 3 teaspoons pureed garlic
- 1 teaspoon turmeric
- ½ teaspoon ground cumin
- 1 teaspoon ground corriander
- 4 tablespoons of oil
- 1 medium tomato chopped
- 1 black cardamom (slightly pounded)

- ¼ teaspoon cumin seeds
- Salt to taste
- 6 cups of water

- 1 green chili seeded and chopped
- 4 tablespoons of chopped cilantro

Save the green chili and the cilantro for later.

Start with boiling the chana and moong daals in a deep pot with the green onions, ginger, garlic, turmeric, cumin, coriander, oil, the chopped tomato, black cardamom, cumin seeds and the salt in 4 cups of water over a medium flame. Partially cover the pot.

Stir initially after 15-20 minutes, at this point add the masoor daal to the pot, cover and continue cooking. Stir periodically (every 3-5 minutes), as the daals cook in the boiling liquid. The liquid in the pot will have a tendency to boil over. Adjust the flame as needed, at the right flame the daals will boil rapidly with the pot covered without boiling over.

Cooking time will vary-usually it takes about an hour. You want to make sure that the lentils are tender. They do need to be slow cooked on a medium to low flame. Check for doneness by taking a small quantity and pressing it between your fingers and thumb. Add more water if needed. Lentils do have a tendency to stick to the bottom of the pan when they are close to being done, so occasional stirring is necessary for the last few minutes of cooking, or keep the flame very low.

Do not let the lentils over dry, finished dish should have the thickness of thick rich soup like consistency. If over dried add some water and stir in well.

Stir in the chopped cilantro and the green chili.

Serve with plain boiled rice or chappati.

When buying daal (lentils) from an Indian or Pakistani food market let the store know you are looking for split and peeled lentils or daal

Tarka or Bhigar Ingredients:

- ½ a sliced onion
- 1 clove of garlic chopped
- 1 teaspoon chopped ginger
- ¼ teaspoon cumin seeds
- 2 tablespoons chopped cilantro
- 6 tablespoons (or more) of oil

Heat oil in a frying pan. Brown the onions in the oil over a medium flame. Add the cumin seeds ginger and garlic to the lightly browned onions and cook for another minute or so. Pour the contents over the daal and garnish with cilantro. Enjoy.

Serves 8-10

Chicken Curry Dishes

There are many different ways to cook 'Chicken Curry'. The variations come sometimes in a minor alteration of ingredients, the steps employed, or a unique 'family twist' to a standard recipe developed somewhere along the line.

At times, just like names given to coffee roasts like French or Vienna, where the beans are still Columbian; the recipe earns a name associated with a particular region of the land where the recipe was perhaps developed. Like the names *Kashmiri korma* or *Mughlai korma*, and no matter what you call it, at the end of the day it is still chicken curry.

And then sometimes the same recipe in the hands of a different cook will result in a variation of the original. I have a selection of some common and popular ways that chicken is enjoyed in the Indian/Pakistani homes, for daily family meals as well as for entertaining and special events.

I can say with confidence, that the recipes you find in this book offer tried, tested and carefully developed instructions to help you succeed at the very first attempt; as has been demonstrated many times over by my students at local culinary colleges where I teach. When put to the test, these students produce outstanding results and yes, at their very first attempt.

Chicken Qorma (murgh ka qorma)

In the Indian/Pakistani cuisine, this chicken recipe is the most traditional of all chicken recipes and a likely pick for a good number of occasions. One unspoken school of thought that prevails in many pockets of the Indo/Pak society commands 'chicken qorma' as a 'must have' on menus for weddings and other important affairs, or the menu is deemed incomplete or lacking.

Qorma sauce:

- ⅓ cup oil
- ½ teaspoon cumin seeds
- 1 black cardamom (available at Indian/Pakistani spice stores)
- 2 medium onions sliced thin
- ½ cup chopped cilantro
- 2 tablespoons chopped ginger
- 1 heaping teaspoon pureed ginger
- 1 heaping teaspoon pureed garlic
- 1 teaspoon salt (or to taste)
- ½ teaspoon cayenne pepper
- ½ teaspoon crushed red pepper
- ¼ teaspoon ground turmeric
- 1 teaspoon ground coriander
- 1 teaspoon ground cumin
- ½ cup yogurt (full cream, blended smooth with a spoon)
- 6-8 pureed medium tomatoes
- (or canned pureed tomatoes
- about 2 ½ cups)

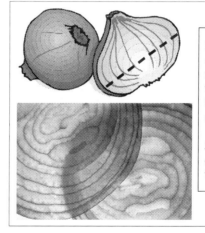

Peel and halve the onions, & then <u>thin</u> slice them width wise in the direction indicated by the dotted line.

Starting at the top end and going to the tail end.

Water as a cooking aid

To sauté the Chicken:
- 1 ½ to 2 lb chicken cut up
  (mostly boneless but some with bones, cut in 1" pieces or as desired)
- 1 tablespoon ginger garlic paste
- ½ teaspoon salt
- ¼ teaspoon crushed red pepper
- 2 tablespoons cilantro
- 2 tablespoons of butter or oil
- ¼ teaspoon of ground turmeric

Qorma sauce

Heat oil in a deep sauce pan, add the cumin seeds and the black cardamom and sauté for a few seconds. Add the sliced onions, two tablespoons of cilantro and two tablespoons of chopped ginger; stir often as you sauté onions. Continue cooking until most of the water from the onions has evaporated and the onions start to turn a light golden color. Cooking time for this step is approximately 15 minutes on a medium flame.

Add the ginger and garlic puree, and another tablespoon or two of the chopped cilantro. Cook for 10 to 15 seconds, until the ginger and garlic start to lend their flavor to the pot. At this point add the salt, cayenne pepper, crushed red pepper, turmeric, ground coriander and the ground cumin and stir into the onion mix. Continue to sauté the spice and onion mixture on a medium flame, stirring to prevent the mixture from sticking to the bottom of the pan. Every 2 or 3 minutes add a few drops of water and continue to sauté on a medium flame.

Repeat this step two or three times. Add yogurt and blend it smooth into the spice mixture. Cook for about another 7-10 minutes. Add the fresh chopped tomatoes or the tomato puree. Stir and cook for 5-7 minutes. Add a cup of water, cover the pot and let cook and simmer on medium low heat.

Keep an eye on the qorma sauce as it is cooking, stir every few minutes to keep it from sticking to the bottom of the pan. If needed, continue to add a few tablespoons of water periodically (5-6 minutes) during this cooking process to keep the sauce from becoming too thick or drying up. Cooking time for this stage may vary; an approximate cooking time is about 15-20 minutes.

To sauté the chicken:

In a separate pan heat oil, or melted butter and add the chicken pieces along with the remaining ingredients. Cook uncovered for even cooking on all sides. Let the water in the pan evaporate. Cooking time will vary, 15 to 20 minutes approximately.

To complete the dish:
Add the cooked chicken to the prepared qorma sauce, fold chicken into the qorma, cover and cook on low heat for about 15-20 minutes, then let simmer on very low heat for 5-7 minutes. Turn heat off, and let dish sit for a few minutes before serving. The meat should have an adequate amount of a rich qorma sauce around it.

Serve with rice and/or chappatis or naan
Serves 8-10

Chicken Karahi

This is a quick curry dish, typically cooked in a wok, but I often cook it in a regular pot as well. It starts initially on a high flame, and towards the end you simmer it on low. I have two versions for a finish on this dish, both included here in the first version (version I) the chicken is directly added to the prepared base sauce, and in the second version (version II) the chicken is marinated first, sautéed in a separate pan and then added to the prepared base sauce to simmer. For the base sauce, *ingredients and steps* are the <u>same</u> for both versions.

A Quick Note:

For Indian/Pakistani chicken dishes almost <u>always</u> use skinless meat. You can use all boneless breasts, or as I often like to add a couple of pieces with the bone in; such as legs, thighs or chicken wings. If you are using a leg or thigh piece, cut it up into 2-3 smaller pieces with a cleaver or a sharp knife so the juices from the bone can lend flavor to the dish. This is strictly optional, and boneless meat by itself will work just fine. Prep all your ingredients before you start and cooking should not take more than 30-45 minutes.

Version I:

- 1 ½ to 2 lbs chicken cut up into 1 ½" pieces.
  (Washed and pat dried.)

For the Curry Sauce:
(same base sauce for version I or version II)

- ⅓ cup cooking oil (I use olive oil)
- A pinch of cumin seeds
- ½ cup finely chopped green onion
- 1 cup chopped cilantro
- 1 heaping teaspoon pureed ginger
- 1 heaping teaspoon pureed garlic
- 1-2 Serrano chilies seeded and chopped
- ½ teaspoon crushed red pepper
- ⅛ teaspoon ground cayenne pepper
- ½ teaspoon ground cumin
- ½ teaspoon ground coriander
- 1 teaspoon salt
- 6-8 medium tomatoes, chopped

- ½ cup canned tomato puree (optional)
- 1 tablespoon dried fenugreek leaves (optional)
  (sold at Indian/Pakistani grocery stores)

- A cup of water on the side as cooking aid

Step One:
Heat oil in a wok or a deep fryer over a medium to medium high flame. Add cumin seeds, green onion, a couple of tablespoons of the chopped cilantro, cook for 2-3 minutes. Add the pureed ginger and garlic and cook for 2-3 minutes stirring constantly. Do not let them turn brown, as soon as they start to have a glazed appearance, add the crushed red pepper, cayenne pepper, ground coriander, cumin and salt.

Step Two:
Cook the spices through, stirring constantly to remove the raw edge of spices, this is an essential step in Indian/Pakistani curry prep; a little close attention and time invested here, will ensure a more delicious final product. The trick here is to sauté the spices in minimal moisture. The spice mixture will have a tendency to stick to the bottom of the pan as the liquid evaporates. Add a few drops of water occasionally to cool the spice mixture as you sauté it, then cook as you continue to stir for another couple of minutes on a medium flame, repeating the process 2-3 times. At this stage add the chopped tomatoes, pureed tomatoes and a couple to tablespoons of the chopped cilantro. Cover and let the tomatoes cook on a medium low flame until they are tender and start to dissolve, about 10-12 minutes.

Step Three:
(to cook version I)
Add the cut-up chicken stir often and make sure all sides of the chicken are cooked through. Cook for about 20 minutes, or until most of the liquid from tomatoes has dried up. At this point you can partially cover the dish, reduce heat and let the dish simmer. Add the prepared Serrano (green) chili, Serrano chili adds more flavor to the dish. Cooking is complete when the oil begins to surface on the sides of the pan. Add the dried fenugreek leaves and fold in the dish. Turn off heat, and let the dish sit for a few minutes before serving.

Garnish with cilantro

Chicken Karahi version II
(steps one and two are the same as for version I)

Step Three:
- 1 ½ to 2 lbs chicken cut up into 1 ½" pieces. (washed and pat dried.)
- ½ teaspoon pureed ginger
- ½ teaspoon pureed garlic
- 2 tablespoon of chopped cilantro
- 2 tablespoon of yogurt (full cream or low fat)
- ½ teaspoon salt
- ½ teaspoon crushed red pepper
- 2 tablespoons oil

For the chicken prep
Add the chicken, ginger, garlic, salt, crushed red pepper, cilantro and yogurt in a deep bowl and let the chicken marinate for 10-15 minutes.

To complete cooking:
Prepare the tomato sauce using steps one and two above. In a separate pan heat oil and add the marinated chicken. Start by cooking the chicken on a high flame uncovered, stirring the chicken for an even sauté of all pieces. Cook for about 10-12 minutes. The chicken will begin to lend its water to the pan, if the liquid is too much, continue to cook to allow most of the liquid to evaporate. Eyeballing for the right consistency and amount of liquid in the pan, continue to cook on a very low flame until the liquid in the pan is mostly dried up, and you are left with just a thin film at the bottom of the pan. Transfer the sautéed chicken to the prepared tomato sauce and fold in. Cover and let cook on a medium low flame. Cooking time may vary between 20-30 minutes; chicken should have a reasonable amount of sauce around it. Simmer partially covered on a very low flame for 10-15 minutes. Add the dried fenugreek leaves; gently fold them in. Turn the stove off cover and let sit for 10-15 minutes before serving.

Garnish with chopped cilantro and thin sliced Serrano chili.

Can be prepared a day before. This dish also freezes well. Great with basmati rice, chappatis or Indian Naans.

Serves 6-8

Chicken Curry

This chicken curry recipe creates a very versatile sauce that can be the base sauce in the preparation of many different dishes, both vegetarian and non-vegetarian.

A do ahead tip and short-cut: Prepare multiple batches of the curry and freeze it in plastic containers in appropriate proportions for one dish, then simply take one portion, warm it up in a pot and add chicken, stewing beef or lamb meat and cook until done . . . dinner is ready in minutes.

For the Curry Sauce:
- 6 tablespoons cooking oil
- ¼ teaspoon cumin seeds
- 1 slightly pounded black cardamom
- 2 medium onions, sliced thin
- 6 tablespoons chopped cilantro
- 1 bunch chopped green onions (optional)
- 2 teaspoons pureed garlic
- 2 teaspoons pureed ginger
- ½ teaspoon ground cumin
- ⅓ teaspoon turmeric
- 1 lightly heaping teaspoon ground coriander
- ½ teaspoon ground chili pepper (cayenne pepper)
- Salt to taste
- 6-8 medium tomatoes chopped
- 1 chopped & seeded Serrano chili
- 2 lbs. boneless chicken breast, cut in 2" pieces (optional: a couple of chicken pieces with the bone)

Garam massala for garnish (optional)

Heat oil in a large frying pan and add cumin seeds, black cardamom and a tablespoon or so of the cilantro; cook for a few seconds (15-20) and then add the sliced regular onions and the chopped green onions.

Cook until most of the water from the onions has evaporated. This can take anywhere from 15-20 minutes depending on the flame and the thickness of the pot. The onions at this point may start to turn a light golden brown. Keep stirring and make sure the onions stay a light golden color.

Add the pureed ginger and garlic, and sauté the mixture as you continue to stir for another couple of minutes. Add the ground cumin, cayenne, turmeric, ground coriander and salt and keep stirring.

Sauté the spices over a medium flame in the mixture for five to six minutes; this is a critical step in preparing a good curry sauce-these spices have to be sautéed well to remove their raw edge and this also brings out their flavor. If the mixture seems to be drying and sticking to the bottom of the pan, keep adding a few drops of water every couple of minutes or as needed. This will lower the temperature of the spice mix, slow down the cooking process for a bit and keep the spices and the curry mixture from sticking to the bottom of the pan. Repeat this step two to three times. Stir often.

Add the chopped tomatoes to the mixture and cook for 5-7 minutes. Add ¾ of the curry mixture to a food processor or a blender and blend to a smooth paste.

Return the sauce to the pot, cook for another few minutes to let some of the water from the tomatoes evaporate, allowing the tomatoes to cook through. (about 15 minutes). Add the prepared cut up chicken and cook for about 10 minutes uncovered, add one cup of water, cover the pot and cook for 30-35 minutes on a medium to medium low flame. Reduce flame and let simmer for another 10-12 minutes, stirring occasionally. Watch for the oil to surface slightly at the edges. Garnish with cilantro, chopped Serrano chili and garam massala. Cover and let the dish rest for a few minutes (8-10) before serving. Serve with rice or chappatis.

Serves: 6-8

Note: finished dish should have a thick and rich soup like sauce around the meat. Adjust flame and liquid as needed as you simmer.

Chicken Keema

(Pan cooked ground chicken)

This recipe is as quick as it can be. I make it often; I will usually leave it as it is outlined below and keep the keema (ground meat) plain. But as a variation you can add 1 cup of peas to the dish towards the end in the last 5 minutes of cooking.

- 4-6 tablespoons oil
- ¼ teaspoon cumin seeds
- 1 tablespoon julienned ginger
- 1 bunch green onions chopped
- ½ cup chopped cilantro
- 1 heaping teaspoon pureed ginger and garlic (see p.217)
- 1 teaspoon salt
- ½ teaspoon crushed red pepper
- 2 lbs Ground chicken white or dark meat
- ¼ teaspoon garam massala

Heat oil in a deep pan over a medium flame; add the cumin seeds and let sizzle for 5-10 seconds. Add the julienned ginger, green onions and half of the chopped cilantro.

Cook the onions for 5-7 minutes (until translucent- but not browned), stir often as you sauté. Add the pureed ginger and garlic, salt and the crushed red pepper and sauté the spice mixture for a few seconds, until the ginger and the garlic begin to lend their aroma. Do not let the ginger/garlic turn brown, just lightly sauté.

Add the ground chicken and the remaining cilantro, stir as you cook to make sure the chicken is folded well into the spice mixture. Keep separating and breaking up the clumping meat. Make sure to sauté the meat evenly on all sides. Cook uncovered for 8-10 minutes, until the ground chicken is cooked through.

Cover the pan, lower the heat and cook for another 10-15 minutes. Partially uncover the pot at this point and add garam massala, then fold in the garam massala and finish cooking with the pot still partially covered allowing any excess liquid to evaporate. Some of the chicken pieces may start to turn a light golden brown at the edges, and the oil may begin to surface in the pot.

Complete cooking by letting the ground chicken sauté on very low heat for 3-5 minutes. Turn off heat, cover and let sit in the pot for a few minutes before serving.

Serves 2-4

Variation to 'Matar Keema', or ground chicken with peas
- 1 ½ cups of peas,
- a pinch of cumin seeds
- 1 teaspoon of oil

Heat the oil in a non stick frying pan, add the cumin seeds and then the peas and give them a quick 2-3 minute sauté on a high flame. Add the sautéed peas to the chicken when the chicken is almost cooked, towards the end as you start to simmer the chicken. Fold in the peas into the ground meat, garnish with some more chopped cilantro if desired and serve.

Serves 2-4

Chicken Stir Fry:
With Vegetables

I am including this recipe here for two reasons:

1) Growing up it was, and still is one of my daughter Naureen's favorite dish
2) It is a real quick dish to fix

Also it adds interest being different.

- ²/₃ cup peeled & sliced carrots
- 1 medium onion peeled and sliced
- 1 10 oz box sliced frozen beans
- ¼ cup slivered toasted almonds
- ²/₃ cup chopped/sliced celery
- 1 medium red bell pepper sliced
- 1 teaspoon crushed or pureed garlic
- ½ teaspoon crushed red pepper
- 1 bunch green onions diced
- 1 tablespoon Butter
- 4 tablespoons olive oil
- 1 ½ lbs diced boneless chicken breast

SAUCE:

- 2 tablespoons corn starch
- 2 chicken flavored bullion cubes
- 3 teaspoons Lemon Juice
- 2 teaspoons lemon peel
- 1 cup boiling water

For the Sauce:

Put half of the water in a bowl and mix in the chicken bullion and the cornstarch until well blended, add the lemon juice, lemon peel and the remaining water and set aside.

For the Chicken and Vegetables:

Stir fry carrots in one tablespoon olive oil and two table spoons of water for a couple of minutes.

Add celery, green onions, bell pepper and beans and cook 2 minutes in a deep pan or a wok. Add two tablespoons water and the butter and coat well, empty wok's contents. Add the remaining oil to the wok, when the oil is hot, add the pureed garlic and let sizzle for a few seconds. Add the green onions, the crushed red pepper and the diced chicken, cook until well done—about 5 to 7 minutes on a medium high flame stirring as you cook to ensure even cooking of all pieces. Cover to steam if necessary for a couple of minutes to cook well. Uncover and add the prepared sauce and continue to cook uncovered on high flame for 2-3 minutes, as soon as the sauce starts to thicken add the cooked vegetables. Stir to fold together the vegetables and the cooked chicken, sprinkle the toasted almonds on the top.

Serve with Steamed or fried rice.

Serves 4-6

Zaffarani Chicken

(Chicken cooked in saffron)

Zaffarani chicken is another one of my mother's specialties; it was usually saved for and served at real special occasions. Chicken is first marinated in yogurt then cooked in an aromatic blend of cardamom and saffron, seasoned with powdered ginger and enriched with butter and almonds. It is great with naan or parathas.

- 2 lbs Boneless Chicken Breast, cut in 2" pieces
- ½ lb chicken wings drumsticks, skin removed
- 1 cup yogurt
- 2 tablespoons butter
- ¼ cup cooking oil
- 4-5 cardamom pods
- ½ cup ground almonds
- ¾ teaspoon powdered ginger
- Salt to taste
- ½ teaspoon Crushed red pepper
- ½ teaspoon saffron threads soaked in ¼ cup of warm milk
- 3 dried red chili peppers

In a mixing bowl marinate the cubed boneless chicken and the chicken wings in yogurt. Set aside for a couple of hours in the refrigerator.

Heat oil and butter in a saucepan. Add the green cardamoms, and let the cardamoms sizzle in hot oil/butter mix for a few seconds. Add the marinated chicken, powdered ginger and salt and cook uncovered on a medium flame. Chicken will begin to lend its water to the pot. Cook for about 15-20 minutes until the chicken has cooked through. Stir often as you cook.

Add the ground almonds and the crushed red pepper. Cover and let simmer on low to medium heat for about 15-20 minutes.

Add the milk with saffron, and simmer, partially uncovered. Cook until most of the water in the pot evaporates and the oil begins to surface around the edges, about 10-12 minutes. Add the 3 whole dried red chili peppers. Cover and let the dish sit for 10-15 minutes before serving.

Transfer to a serving dish, garnish with cilantro if desired.

Serves 8

Chicken Pot Roast with Lemon and Ginger

This recipe was perhaps inspired by the British Cuisine, and made its way into the Indian kitchens during the 'British Raj' in India. I grew up loving this dish, and it was a favorite one with my siblings as well. We all looked forward to the night 'ginger chicken roast' would be on the menu. The flavor is amazing. It is seasoned with green chili, ginger and lemon and is simply a treat. The best part is, it's a cinch to fix.

- 1 whole chicken
  (skin removed and giblets removed from the cavity)
- 2" piece of peeled fresh ginger
- 4 Serrano green chilies, seeded
- ½ cup lemon juice
- 1 teaspoon salt for the marinade
- 1 teaspoon salt to rub the body cavity
- ¼ cup oil
- 6-8 baby potatoes, cleaned and dried,
  (or 2-4 medium size white potatoes cut in large wedges)
- 8-10 baby onions peeled and kept whole
- ½ cups green peas

Directions:

To prepare the marinade, blend together the ginger, green chilies, lemon juice and one measure of salt in the container of a food processor or a blender and blend to a smooth paste. Wash and pat dry the chicken and rub the chicken body cavity with the 2nd measure of salt. Put little cuts and nicks all over the chicken meat with the tip of a sharp knife or a fork to prepare for marinating.

Place chicken in a deep bowl or a dish and rub gently all over with the contents of the blender. Cover the bowl with plastic and let it marinate for 2-4 hours inside the refrigerator.

Heat oil in a heavy large skillet, as the oil heats up gently place the chicken in the pot on its back first and let it cook a few minutes (3-5) till it browns lightly. Turn the chicken upside down, alternating sides to brown both the right and left halves of the breast meat. Sear each side of the breast meat for 3-4 minutes. Cover the skillet, slightly reducing heat and cook for 12-15 minutes. Turning sides once or twice for even cooking.

Add the potatoes and the onions, cover and let cook for another 20-30 minutes, once again turning the chicken as needed. If the contents seem to begin to dry too much, sprinkle with just a few drops of water. When the chicken is just about done, add the peas to the pot partially uncover the pot and finish cooking on a low flame. Stir as needed.

Garnish with the vegetables in the pot, serve with rice or chappatis.

Serves 4-6

A quick Chicken Massala Stir fry

Serves Two

A quick version of a fast cooking stir fried curry designed to serve two. The real work is in the prep, and then cooking takes just a few minutes. You can also marinate the chicken pieces in a couple of tablespoons of yogurt and some salt for 30 minutes to an hour before cooking, that adds a certain softness and creaminess to the meat. The version below without the yogurt marinade comes out just as delicious.

- 2 tablespoons olive oil
- ¼ teaspoon cumin seeds
- 1 tablespoon julienned ginger
- 2 tablespoons chopped cilantro
- 2 teaspoons pureed ginger and garlic (see p. 217)
- ¼ teaspoon crushed red pepper
- ¼ teaspoon cayenne pepper
- Salt to taste
- ½ a bunch chopped green onion
- 1 pound boneless chicken breast cut in 1" pieces or
- 1 lb chicken tenders
- 2 Roma tomatoes chopped
- ¼ cup chunked red bell pepper
- Water as cooking aid

In a deep large frying pan heat oil over a medium flame. Add the cumin seeds, julienned ginger and cilantro, and sauté for 15-20 seconds, next add the pureed ginger and garlic, and continue to sauté the mix for an additional 15 seconds. Next add the crushed red pepper, cayenne pepper and salt, sauté the spices in the herb mixture for 7-9 minutes, stirring often and adding a few drops of water as needed to keep the contents from sticking to the bottom of the pan or burning. Add the green onion and the prepared chicken; cook chicken on medium flame, stirring as you cook for an even cooking. About 15 minutes.

Reduce flame, circle the chicken around the edge of the pan to make some room in the middle of the pan and add the tomatoes and some additional ginger and garlic if desired, and a tablespoon of chopped cilantro.

Cook uncovered for 5 minutes, then cover and let cook for another 15 minutes or so, eyeballing the mix, to see if most of the water in the pan has dried up, and the oil has started to surface. At this point add the bell peppers, and cook partially covered for 3-5 minutes on a very low heat.

Let simmer for another couple of minutes for a richer consistency. Enjoy with rice, Chappati or I will even serve it with some prepared pasta of your choice.

Serves 2-4

Whole Wheat Pasta with Stir Fry Chicken

Desi (i.e. Indian/Pakistani) style

Again, I am including this dish here for a similar reason like the stir fry chicken recipe, where on occasions I will take a dish from another cuisine, and give it a little bit of an Indian/Pakistani twist, if you will. I often did this when the kids were growing up with dishes from other cuisines that they enjoyed.

CHICKEN TOPPING

- One piece Chicken breast; flattened by pounding slightly with a meat pounder, between sheets of wax/parchment paper
- olive oil spray
- 1 bunch chopped green onion
- 5 cloves of garlic crushed/pureed
- 4 tablespoons chopped cilantro
- 1 teaspoon crushed red pepper
- ¼ teaspoon ground cumin
- ½ tablespoon salt
- ¼ thin sliced green bell pepper
- ¼ yellow bell pepper
- ½ teaspoon ground black pepper or lemon pepper
- 4 tablespoons Olive Oil
- ¼ cup crumbled feta cheese

PASTA:
10-12 cups of water
- 1 package whole wheat pasta, 16 oz box
- 1 teaspoon salt
- 2 cups chopped lettuce
- 1 carrot peeled and sliced in thin diagonal slices

- 2 tablespoons olive oil
- ½ t spoon lemon pepper

MARINARA SAUCE:

- 1 32 oz jar any good quality pasta sauce, any flavor of your choice

For the chicken

Lightly spray a frying pan with the olive oil spray, lightly brown chicken on both sides, and squirt with additional dash of the olive oil spray as needed for the other side. Drain chicken on an absorbent paper plate or on paper towel. Slice chicken in thin strips when cool enough to handle.

Heat the olive oil in a deep pan or pot, add the chopped green onions to the oil, sauté for a minute or so, without letting them brown, add the garlic and a little bit of the chopped cilantro, cook for another minute and add the crushed red pepper, salt and the ground cumin. Cook the spices stirring constantly for a minute or so, and then add the sliced chicken, stir the chicken to coat well with the ingredients in the pan and let cook for another 2-3 minutes. Add the sliced bell peppers, lemon pepper and the remaining cilantro, stirring to fold all ingredients for a minute, turn the heat off and add the feta cheese, set aside.

For the Pasta:

Boil water in a deep pot, add salt and the pasta when the water begins to boil, cover and let cook for about ten minutes, or till the pasta appears done. Drain the pasta in a colander and return back to the pot, add the lettuce, sliced carrots, lemon pepper and the olive oil to the pasta and stir to coat on low heat, turn off heat.

For the Sauce:

Warm up the sauce in a pot; add a little oil and garlic to the sauce, if desired.

To serve:

Put the prepared pasta into a serving platter, pour the sauce on top, and spoon the cooked chicken over the spaghetti and the sauce. Garnish with cilantro and a little more crumbled feta, and enjoy.

Serves 4-6

From The Grill

**Grilling
Tandoori Chicken
During a Cooking Class**

Grilled food is absolutely hands down my favorite. Sometimes on days that I have been cooking a lot, let's say for when I may be fixing food to entertain friends or family. My focus on cooking and event prep will at times curb my appetite-and trust me only *temporarily*. (Pardon the disappointment; but there are no 'diet' fads I am offering here). At the end of the day I am from a 'Kashmiri' family, and you can't keep us *Kashmiris* away from food too long. The only time this transitory phenomenon does not kick in is when I am GRILLING-this is when I can cook and be hungry all at the same time.

I am including some favorite and popular grilling recipes here from the Indian/ Pakistani cuisine. Including some favorites served at tikka and kabob houses all over the city, from fancy restaurants to tikka corners around town.

Ground Chicken Seekh Kabobs

The trick in making these kabobs is mastering the art of wrapping your meat around the skewer. You want an even spread of meat, not too thick a layer so it cooks evenly. If the layer is too thick it will look grilled on the outside with grill marks and all, but the inside portion closer to the metal of the skewer may still be left uncooked. For any meat and especially with chicken you want the meat well cooked for health reasons alone.

- 2 lbs ground chicken dark meat
- ½ cup chopped cilantro
- 1 bunch green onions finely chopped
- 1 tablespoon garam massala (store bought or home made)*
- 2-4 Serrano chilies seeded and chopped
- 2 tablespoons pureed ginger and garlic (see p. 217)
- 1 teaspoon crushed red pepper
- 1 teaspoon salt
- 1 teaspoon heavy whipping cream

*See chapter on Spices for garam massala recipe (p. xxxi)

To season and marinate the ground meat:
Fold together the herbs, spices and the cream in a large bowl add the ground meat to the spice mix and combine the ingredients well with your hands.

Cover the mix and let it sit in the refrigerator for a few minutes. (meat should be well chilled)

Forming kabobs:

You can wrap the seasoned ground meat directly on a metal skewer and grill it over live flames. What I often do is, first, wrap a thin strip of foil around a metal skewer and then spread the meat over the foil. Next, I gently remove the foil, wrapped with meat, off the skewer and place it on a cookie sheet. I repeat the process until all of my kabobs are formed and ready to be grilled. This allows me to barbeque them all at the same time. The grilling time for the pre-spread kabobs is no more than 15-20 minutes.

Aids to form kabobs:
  i)   Glass of cold water
  ii) 12 to 14 strips of foil (About 3" W X 12" L, or the average length of the roll)
  iii) A metal skewer or pre-soaked bamboo skewers
  iv) A large cookie sheet lined with foil

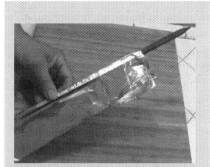

Figure 1 dressing the skewer

Figure 2: tightening foil around the skew

Figure 3: wrapping meat around the skewer

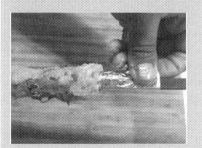

Fig 4: removing formed kabob from the skewer

DRESSING THE SKEWER WITH FOIL:

Wrapping a sheet of foil around the skewer:

Take a cut sheet of foil (3"x 12") and place the skewer in the Middle of the sheet along the length of the piece (Fig 1), press foil along the middle of the skewer to form a crease, tighten the crease so it's snug around the skewer. Rotate the skewer clockwise, holding the top folded portion of the foil and wrapping the foil at the same time over the skewer in an anti clockwise motion, tightening the foil piece around the skewer as you go.
See (Fig 2)

Once the skewer is dressed up with foil, you can now spread the meat over it to form the kabob (Fig 3)

To form kabobs:

Take a fist full of the ground meat mix and wrap it over the foil covered skewer. (see directions on dressing the skewer above)*,

Dip your hands in cold water as you continue to spread the meat along the length of the skewer. (Fig 3) Leave a one inch piece of the foil at both ends uncovered.

Next, remove the wrapped kabob from the skewer by holding the top end of the foil and gently pulling it off the skewer; place it on the prepared cookie sheet. (Fig 4)

The foil the kabob is wrapped over now acts as the 'skewer' for the kabob. Repeat the steps, wrapping foil first around the skewer and then covering it with the meat until all kabobs are formed.

Let the kabobs air dry for about 5-10 minutes then cover with plastic wrap or foil and refrigerate the formed kabobs until ready to grill or broil. Kabobs can be formed and refrigerated up to a day ahead.

This technique of forming kabobs saves time and divides the work into two easy steps; as once all the kabobs are formed you can grill them all at the same time. Usually the grilling time is about 10-15 minutes.

Out-door Grilling:
Grill on medium flame (gas or charcoal) turning as needed, approximately 2-4 minutes for each side so that all sides are evenly cooked.

Indoor Broiling:
Pre-heat the oven broiler, Place a wire rack on a cookie sheet and line the kabobs on top. Slide them in the oven placing them on the rack closest to the broiler flame. Let broil a few minutes on each side, turning for even browning. To turn the kabobs over, remove the cookie sheet from the oven, turn over each kabob using a pair of tongs, slide the cookie sheet back in the oven to cook the uncooked side. Once cooked on all sides remove from oven and let cool for a couple of minutes, slide off the foil before serving.

Removing kabobs from the foil:
Hold a bare end of foil in one hand and with the other hand hold the edge of the kabob nearest to the held end of the foil, gently slide the kabob off the foil, the kabob should slip off with ease. Repeat for all. You can cut each full length kabob into half or thirds for serving.

Garnish with onion, tomato and cilantro before serving.

Yields 12-15 kabobs

Ground Beef Seekh Kabobs

Serves 6-8

At a first glance this recipe or the ground chicken kabob recipe (preceding) may appear somewhat involved, but I promise you both these recipes are quick and simple. These kabobs come out great whether you broil them in your oven or grill them out doors. They can be cooked an hour or two before serving place them in a shallow dish or a skillet, cover them tightly with foil to keep them moist and warm, and then reheat them for a few seconds if needed in a microwave before serving.

- 2 to 2 ½ lbs ground beef (ideally fresh not frozen)
- ½ cup chopped cilantro
- 1 bunch green onions finely chopped (both the dark and light green parts)
- 1 tablespoon garam massala*
- 4-6 Serrano chilies seeded and chopped
- 1 tablespoon pureed ginger
- 1 tablespoon pureed garlic
- 1 teaspoon crushed red pepper
- 1 teaspoon salt or to taste
- 1 teaspoon heavy whipping cream

* For homemade garam massala see page 215, or the chapter on spices

To season and marinate the ground meat:
Fold together the herbs, spices and the 1 teaspoon cream in a large bowl, now add the ground meat and mix the ingredients well with your hands. Cover the mix and let it sit in the refrigerator for a few minutes. (meat should be well chilled)

Aids to forming kabobs:
Please look under recipe for 'Ground Chicken Kabobs'

DRESSING THE SKEWER WITH FOIL:
See recipe for Ground Chicken Kabobs

To form kabobs:
For directions please look under recipe for Ground Chicken Kabobs

Out Door Grilling:
See recipe for 'Ground Chicken Kabobs'

Indoor Broiling:
See recipe for 'Ground Chicken Kabobs'

Removing kabobs from the foil before serving:
See recipe for 'Ground Chicken Kabobs'

Yield: 14-18 kabobs

Tandoori Chicken on the Grill

When I use chicken breasts for this recipe, with or without bone, I usually 'butterfly' the piece to get a thinner cut of meat. That helps to marinate the meat well, adding flavor and richness to every morsel, also ensures even and fast cooking. I love '*tandoori chicken*' and can have it for dinner every night. At my café, I served it packed inside a naan dressed with chutney and grilled onions for a delicious sandwich. It was one of the most popular items on our menu . . .

- 2-3 lbs Chicken cut up
  (you can use boneless chicken breasts or thighs, or breast halves with bone-in or leg and thigh quarters)

All chicken used is skinless. Poke chicken pieces with a fork or make deep cuts in the meat with the tip of a sharp knife.

- 2 cups yogurt
- 1 tablespoon pureed ginger and
- 1 tablespoon pureed garlic
- 1 slightly heaping tablespoons garam massala*
  (store bought or homemade)
- ¾ teaspoon cayenne pepper
- 1 tablespoons yellow food color (optional)
- ½ teaspoon egg yellow food color (optional)
- ¼ cup oil
- ¼ cup chopped cilantro
- ½ a bunch chopped green onion
- salt to taste

* For homemade garam massala recipe look under chapter on spices

Directions:

Mix all of the above ingredients (except for the cilantro and the chopped green onion) in a large mixing bowl. Add the chicken pieces and make sure the marinade is gently rubbed deep into the cuts made in the meat and that all the meat is well coated with the yogurt based marinade. Top with the chopped cilantro and the chopped green onion. Cover tightly with plastic wrap and refrigerate.
Marinate for 2-4 hours or overnight.

Grilling Aids:
A cup of oil and a pastry brush

Grilling: Clean and preheat the grill, brush the grill lightly with oil. If the grill is pre-heated on a high flame I will usually try to cool the grill slightly by using moist/water soaked paper towels and then brush the grill with oil.

Place chicken pieces on the prepared grill and cook on low flame for about 10-12 minutes on one side, the cooking time for each side is best determined by the size and performance of each grill, a good practice would be to check periodically during cooking. Turn chicken pieces for even cooking on all sides, you want to cook it on a medium to medium-low flame so the meat cooks through. Brush chicken with oil while cooking to keep meat from drying up, especially the white meat.

Garnish with Lemon, sliced onions and cilantro! Serve with chutney and naan. Enjoy . . .

6-8 Servings

Steps to butterfly the boneless breast of Chicken:

Butterflying the chicken breast lends the meat a workable thickness for quick and even cooking. It also helps the meat to marinate well at the same time.

1

Take a sharp kitchen knife, and starting from the narrow end of the breast slice halfway through the thickness of the chicken, keeping your knife parallel to the cutting surface.

2

Cut the meat almost all the way through and stop at about ½" from the end of the breast.

3

Open the sliced top fillet of the breast like flipping the page of a book and now you have one large piece.

Easy Chicken Tikka

This dish is not only unbelievably healthy and nutritious, but amazingly delicious. After grilling or broiling it, you can enjoy it rolled in a whole wheat pita or naan, with some chopped tomatoes, lettuce, cucumber and mint chutney, or with some pan grilled sliced bell peppers and onions either way it is delightful. Often I will also serve it with whole wheat spaghetti, with some vegetables tossed in it or with just some plain basmati rice. The serving options are only limited to your preference and imagination.

I strongly believe that healthy choices in food are way more appetizing than unhealthy ones.

- 2-4 boneless skinless chicken breasts
- Juice of one lemon fresh squeezed (remove or strain all seeds)
- grated rind of one lemon
- 1 teaspoon salt or to taste
- 1 teaspoon fresh ground black pepper
- ½ teaspoon crushed red pepper
- ¼ teaspoon ground red pepper
- ¼ onion pureed
- 1 slightly heaping teaspoon pureed ginger
- 1 slightly heaping teaspoon pureed garlic
- 2 tablespoons chopped cilantro
- 2 tablespoons olive oil
- ½ cup yogurt

Grilling Aids:
- ¼ cup oil
- A pastry brush

Wash and pat dry the chicken pieces and if using breast pieces with or without the bone, thin slice or butterfly* the chicken breast pieces, this will allow the meat to marinate and grill evenly.

In a deep bowl mix in the lemon juice, the lemon rind, ground black pepper, crushed red pepper, ground red pepper, salt, ginger, garlic, onion, cilantro and mix well. Add the yogurt and the olive oil to the mixture in the bowl and blend well. Put tiny cuts on the meat pieces with the tip of a sharp knife and add to the marinade, coat well and marinate for 1-2 hours.

To Grill:
Clean and pre heat the grill, brush the grill rods lightly with oil. Place chicken pieces on the grill. Cook 4-6 minutes on each side.

Turn chicken pieces for even cooking on all sides, you want to cook it on a medium to medium-low flame so the meat cooks through. Brush chicken with oil while cooking to keep meat from drying up, especially when cooking white meat.

Repeat turning the meat for even cooking, until the chicken is cooked through.

*See instructions to butterfly chicken under:
'Tandoori Chicken on the Grill'

Serves 4-6

Grilled Tandoori Lamb Chops

I love lamb chops, grilled or cooked in a curry sauce, with or without vegetables. Lamb chops are an expensive cut of meat; there are some smaller ethnic markets, however, that usually offer them at a lower price. One of the markets that I go to in my area generally brings a whole rack of lamb from the freezer for me and I request them to give me a slightly thicker cut, approximately 1"-1 ½" in thickness. I like them cut thicker so the chops remain moist and do not dry out when grilled. Of course, the level of flame and the duration of cooking will play a role here as well, but the first step is to start out with a slightly plump lamb chop.

- 8-10 lamb chops
- 1 heaping teaspoon pureed ginger
- 1 heaping teaspoon pureed garlic
- 1 teaspoon garam massala
- 1 teaspoon salt
- juice of half a lemon
- ½ teaspoon crushed red pepper
- ¼ cup finely chopped green onions
- 2 tablespoons chopped cilantro
- 1/2 cup yogurt (full cream)
- ¼ cup olive oil or grape seed oil
- ¼ teaspoon ground red pepper

Wash and pat dry the lamb chops and set aside, trimming most of the excess fat from the meat side of the chop, except for a thin film to hold the meat together, and set aside.

Mix all of the above remaining ingredients in a mixing bowl, and mix well. Add the lamb chops to the mix. Fold in the lamb chops and make sure to coat well. Cover and refrigerate the marinade for 4-6 hours.

Grilling Lamb Chops:

You will need paper towels, a sponge, some oil in a container and a pastry brush for the grill prep and grilling.

Grill Prep: Brush off any burnt residue and wipe off the grill rods with a stack of wet paper towels or sponge. Preheat the grill; protect your hands if cleaning heated grill rods. I usually let my gas BBQ grill preheat for about 10-15 minutes, if the grill rods seem too hot bring them to a lower temperature by lowering the heat for a few minutes.

Lightly brush the grill rods with oil.

To Grill:

Layer the lamb chops on the prepared grill. Cover and cook for 5-7 minutes, then turn the chops over. Brush the grilled side lightly with oil, cover and grill the flipped side for 4-6 minutes. Check every 2-4 minutes to ensure even grilling, adjusting the position of the chops over the flame individually if needed. Eyeball the meat as you grill to have better control over the cooking process.

This is a great recipe, any leftover chops can be refrigerated or frozen and taste just the same when warmed up.

Serves 4-6

Tandoori Chicken Sandwich

Use your leftover grilled tandoori chicken from last night for these sandwiches, and the best part is it will never taste like leftovers. This recipe lends it a *fresh* new flavor.

- 2 boneless chicken breasts
  (Marinated and grilled following the chicken tikka or tandoori chicken recipes in this book)
- 1 tablespoon oil
- ½ teaspoon pureed ginger and garlic (see p. 217)
- ½ cup onion thin sliced
- ¼ cup chopped cilantro
- ½ cup red bell pepper thin sliced
- ½ cup yellow bell pepper thin sliced
- ½ cup green bell pepper thin sliced
- ½ bunch chopped green onions

• Store bought pita bread or naan
Prepare mint chutney raita dressing from the recipe under 'Chutneys & Raitas' see page 26.

Slice the grilled chicken into thin strips and set aside. In a deep frying pan heat oil and add the pureed ginger and garlic to the pan. Let the ginger and garlic sizzle in the hot oil for 5-7 seconds. Add the sliced onions and a couple of tablespoons of the chopped
cilantro. Let the onions sauté for a couple of minutes. Add the sliced bell peppers, the green onions and the remaining chopped cilantro. Fold the vegetables together. Quickly sauté for a minute or so. Do not over cook. The bell peppers should remain crisp and firm. Add the sliced cooked chicken, folding it into the cooking vegetables.

Warm up a pita or naan. Add a desired amount of the prepared tandoori chicken and vegetable mix. Top with a couple of tablespoons of mint chutney dressing. Wrap the bread around the filling and enjoy.

Makes 4 sandwiches

Seekh Kabob Sandwich

I used to make these sandwiches for my children's lunch boxes to take to school, only to find out years later that often they were traded for peanut butter and jelly sandwiches in their friend's lunch boxes . . . This was shared with me by the same friends who looked forward to the trade, and now occasionally call me seeking a 'kabob sandwich party' at our place. As long as my kids are not calling all over asking for *peanut butter sandwich* parties I know this recipe tested well.

- 6 pieces of grilled ground chicken or beef seekh kabobs
  (See: ground chicken kabob and/ or ground beef kabob recipe)
- 1 tablespoon oil
- ¼ teaspoon pureed ginger
- ¼ teaspoon pureed garlic
- ½ cup onion thin sliced
- ¼ cup chopped cilantro
- ½ cup red bell pepper thin sliced
- ½ cup yellow bell pepper thin sliced
- ½ cup green bell pepper thin sliced
- ½ bunch chopped green onion

Store bought pita bread or naan
Prepare mint chutney raita dressing from the recipe under 'Chutneys & Raitas'

Set aside the grilled kabobs. In a deep frying pan heat oil and add the pureed ginger and garlic to the pan. Let the ginger and garlic sizzle in the hot oil for 5-7 seconds and add the sliced onions and a couple of tablespoons of the chopped cilantro, let the onions sauté for a couple of minutes. Add all of the sliced bell peppers, green onions and the remaining chopped cilantro. Fold the vegetables together. Quick sauté the bell peppers for a minute or so, do not over cook them. They should remain crisp and firm.

Warm up a pita or naan, placing a kabob on the naan and adding a desired serving of the pan grilled vegetable mix. Top with a couple of tablespoons of mint chutney dressing; wrap the bread around the filling and enjoy.

Makes 6 sandwiches

Some Lamb and Beef Dishes

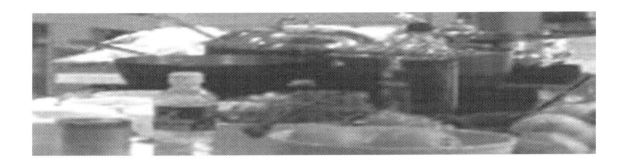

Almost all of the recipes I am including in this section call for lamb or goat, as these are the preferred meats in Indian/Pakistani cuisine, and the most expensive of all the red meats. Using beef is somehow considered a lesser choice and to some extent even looked down upon or regarded equivalent to cutting corners.

I am not going to get into the cultural or historical reasons for this preference, which is not important here, for one reason or the other lamb and goat is the prevalent choice with connoisseurs in the sub-continent, but with that said, beef can be substituted for any recipe that calls for lamb, if you prefer.

Most of the recipes in this section will be great with rice or chappatis.

Lamb Cooked with spinach

(Palak Gosht)

A popular choice for special occasions and wedding menus, this is truly a 'Gourmet' option for its taste, flavor and aroma. It is one of the best ways I know of enjoying spinach and a very desirable preference for entertaining and everyday meals. Try last night's leftover spinach for a Sunday breakfast with *parathas (p.178)*, and life will suddenly hold a new meaning. The combination is irresistible. I am using meat from the leg of lamb for this dish, lamb chops would be another great option.

- 1/3 cup oil
- ½ teaspoon cumin seeds
- 1 black cardamom
- 2 medium onions thin sliced
- 2-4 tablespoons chopped cilantro
- 8 cloves of garlic pureed
- 1 ½" piece of fresh ginger root pureed
- 1 teaspoon cayenne pepper
- 1/2 teaspoon turmeric
- 1 teaspoon ground coriander
- 1 teaspoon ground cumin
- 1 teaspoon (or to taste) salt
- 4 medium tomatoes chopped
- 2 1/2 lbs. lamb leg cut up
  (Cut in 1½" inch cubes, some pieces with the bone-in)
- 2-3 cups water for cooking meat
- 2-10oz. packages of spinach, cooked in boiling water for about 15 minutes and drained completely (or microwave the spinach for 6 minutes in a glass bowl, with a couple of tablespoons of water and covered with a moist paper towel)

- • 1 whole Serrano chili
- • 2 tablespoons dried fenugreek leaves (Optional)*

*(available at most Indian/Pakistani Food Stores labeled as 'Qasuri (Kasoori) Methi', as it comes from a city named Qasoor/Kasoor)
• Water as cooking aid

Heat oil in a saucepan over a medium flame. Add the cumin seeds and the large black cardamom, cook for a few seconds just enough for the spices to lend their flavor to the oil, next add the sliced onions and the chopped cilantro. Sauté the onions till they turn a light golden brown, about 20 minutes keeping an eye on them and stirring them for an even very light browning. At this point add the pureed ginger and garlic and stir for a minute or two.

Add the cayenne pepper, turmeric, salt, ground coriander and the ground cumin to the pot and stir. Cook the spices, to sauté them well, adding a few drops of water every 2-4 minutes or as needed, to keep the mixture from overcooking, burning and sticking to the bottom of the pan. Cook the spice mixture for a good 15 minutes. Add the chopped tomatoes cook them for about 7-10 minutes until they begin to dissolve. Add the meat plus about two tablespoons of cilantro.

Braise the meat for 15-20 minutes approximately; following the same steps used to sauté the spices above, adding a little water when the liquid in the pot begins to evaporate. Searing the meat in the spice mixture helps eliminate odor from the meat. This step is complete once most of the water in the pot is dried up and the oil begins to surface around the edges.

Add 3 cups of water to the pot, cover and let it cook on a medium flame for about 30-35 minutes until most of the water has dried out and the meat has tenderized. Add the spinach, cover and simmer for about another 20 minutes. Fold in the fenugreek leaves and add the serrano chilies. Uncover and simmer to evaporate any excess water, stirring as you simmer until the oil begins to surface. This should take another 10 minutes. (The time given for each step is approximate, and may vary a little depending on the flame and the thickness of the pot, so eyeballing the dish is important, as you may need to adjust the flame to control the cooking process). Partially cover the pot and let it rest for about 5 minutes before serving.

Serves 8-10

Aloo Gosht

Potatoes cooked in lamb

This is for the *'meat and potato'* lovers. How about some meat and potato a little spiced up the Indian/Pakistani way? This dish can be served with rice or chappati, it works well with both.

For the base sauce:

- ½ cup oil
- ½ teaspoon cumin seeds
- 1 black cardamom
- 2 medium onions, sliced
- 1 tablespoon julienned ginger root
- ½ cup chopped cilantro
- 1 heaping teaspoon pureed ginger root
- 1 heaping teaspoon pureed garlic
- 1 teaspoon cayenne pepper (leveled)
- 1/2 teaspoon turmeric
- 1 teaspoon (or to taste) salt
- 1 teaspoon ground coriander
- 1 teaspoon ground cumin
- 6-8 medium size Tomatoes-chopped
- 2 lbs. meat from leg of lamb
  (Cut in 1½" inch cubes, with the bone)*
- 2 ½ cups of water
- 1 whole Serrano chili
- Also some additional water as cooking aid in sautéing the spices and the meat.

* Meat departments at markets and butcher shops will gladly cut the meat for you

For the Potatoes:
- 4-5 Yukon gold potatoes
  (Washed cut in wedges and soaked in water for half an hour)
- 2-4 tablespoons of oil to sauté the potatoes
- A pinch of cumin seeds
- A pinch of salt
- 1 tablespoon chopped cilantro

To Cook the base sauce and the meat:
In a deep pan, heat oil over a medium flame and add the cumin seeds, black cardamom, the sliced onion, julienned ginger and a couple of tablespoons of the chopped cilantro. Sauté the onions until they turn a very light golden brown, about 20 minutes keeping an eye on them and stirring them for even browning. At this point add the pureed ginger and garlic and stir for a minute or two.

Add the cayenne pepper, turmeric, salt, ground coriander and the ground cumin to the pot and stir. Cook the spices, to sauté them well, adding a few drops of water every 2-4 minutes or as needed, to keep the mixture from overcooking, scorching or sticking to the bottom of the pan. Cook them for a good 12-15 minutes. Add the chopped tomatoes and cook the tomatoes for about 15-20 minutes; add the meat plus about two tablespoons of cilantro.

Cook the meat uncovered in the tomato and spice mixture stirring often, the idea of this step is to sear the meat in the spice mixture so the meat absorbs the flavor from the spice mixture and at the same time to remove the raw meat odor. If the spice mixture seems to be drying up too much as you are sautéing the meat, keep adding a few tablespoons of water to the pot every few minutes to keep the mixture moist. Cook the meat in the tomato and spice mixture for 15-20 minutes

Note:

The finished dish typically has a soup like sauce around the meat and vegetable. If the sauce seems too thick you can dilute it by adding some warm water when you combine the two together for the last step of cooking. It is ideal to adjust the liquid while the dish is on simmer.

Add the measured (2½ cups) water, lower the flame, cover the pot and continue cooking the meat for 20-25 minutes.

To Sauté Potatoes:

In a separate pan, heat the oil and add the potatoes along with tablespoon of chopped cilantro, cumin seeds and salt and sauté the potatoes on a low flame until they turn a light golden color on all sides.

Combining the meat and the potatoes:

Add the sautéed potatoes to the meat in the pot. Cook the meat and potatoes on a low flame until the potatoes and meat are tender and done.

Serve with rice or any Indian/Pakistani flat bread.

Serves 6-8

Bhindi Gosht

(okra cooked in meat)

When I cook okra with meat I prefer to use lamb chops-just a preference of mine. It also comes out great with meat from the leg of lamb cut up in 1 ½" to 2" pieces. Ask the butcher to remove any excess fat on the outside and cut up the leg of lamb for you <u>with</u> the bone, a little bit of bone left in with the meat will enhance the flavor of the dish

For the meat base prep
- ¼ cup oil
- ½ teaspoon cumin seeds
- 1 black cardamom
- 1 tablespoon julienned fresh ginger
- 2 medium onions slices thin
- 4 tablespoons chopped cilantro
- 2 heaping teaspoons pureed ginger and garlic (see p. 217)
- ¾ teaspoon ground red pepper (cayenne)
- ¼ teaspoon turmeric powder
- 1 teaspoon ground coriander
- ½ teaspoon ground cumin powder
- 1 teaspoon salt or to taste
- 6-8 tomatoes seeded and chopped
- 2 lbs lamb chops or leg of lamb cut up in 1" to 1½" cubes
- 1½ cups water

For the Okra prep
- 2 lbs fresh okra washed and dried on paper towels-
- outer edge of the stems removed and larger pieces cut in half
- 1 teaspoon ginger and garlic puree (see p. 217)
- ½ teaspoon crushed red pepper
- 1 dash of salt
- 2 tablespoons oil
- 2 chopped Roma tomatoes

133

Heat oil in a cooking pot over a medium flame. When the oil is heated up add the cumin seeds, the black cardamom, julienned ginger and a tablespoon of the chopped cilantro and sauté for a few seconds. Add the sliced onions and sauté the onion mixture until the onions start to turn a light golden brown in color, about 20 minutes keeping an eye on them and stirring them for an even browning. Add the pureed ginger and garlic and stir for a minute or two, until they start to lend their aroma to the pot.

Now, add the cayenne pepper, turmeric, salt, ground coriander and the ground cumin to the browning onions and sauté them for a few minutes to remove the raw edge from the spices. Add a few drops of water every 2-4 minutes or as needed. Stir often to keep the mixture from overcooking, burning or sticking to the bottom of the pan; sauté the spices for a good 15 minutes. Add the chopped tomatoes and cook the tomatoes for about 15-20 minutes.

Once the tomatoes have cooked through and most of he water from the tomatoes is dried up add the meat to the pot and about two tablespoons of cilantro. With the pot uncovered, sauté the meat in the spice mixture for about 10-15 minutes. Add water, cover the pot and let the meat cook on a medium low flame until tender, stir occasionally as you cook. The cooking time here should be between 20-25 minutes.

To Sauté the Okra:
While the meat is cooking, start to sauté the okra in a separate deep fry pan. Add oil to the pan add the prepared okra, red pepper, ginger garlic and the salt and sauté on high heat, stirring constantly to cook evenly on all sides, about 7-10 minutes. Add the chopped tomatoes and continue to sauté for another 3-6 minutes. (stir often for just a light sauté of okra, where the vegetable still maintains most of its green color, it's cooking will complete when combined and simmered with the meat in the next step)

Combining sautéed okra with the cooked meat:
Uncover the pot and check the meat for doneness, meat should be tender and break easy with a spoon. Also as a sign of being done, the oil begins to

surface around the edges of the pot. Add the fried okra to the meat pot and gently fold okra into the meat, so as to allow the sauce in the pan coat the sautéed okra, partially cover and let the dish simmer on a low flame for 8-10 minutes. Turn the flame off; let the cooked dish sit for a few minutes before transferring it to a serving dish.

Serve with rice or chappati.

Serves 6-8

Haleem

Haleem is a great option when entertaining a crowd. Talk about a *desi* brunch (pronounced: 'deh-see'; an intimate slang, that expatriates from the Indo/Pak sub continent use for themselves. Its literal meaning is: one who is from the old county) and you can't go wrong opting to serve *haleem with naans*. Just make sure not to skip the finale of the grilled onion topping, i.e. *tarka* or *bhigar*, and you have a winner at your hands. The use of cracked wheat enhances the volume of this dish, so yield from preparing a single recipe can serve many. Meats and daals are first cooked separately and then brought together for a slow simmer on low heat. The addition of cracked wheat lends starchiness to the dish. The final dish will have an almost thick soup-like consistency.

Haleem with sautéed onion topping (bhigar)

Ingredients:

- ¼ cup oil
- ⅛ teaspoon cumin seeds
- 1 black cardamom
- 2 tablespoons julienned ginger
- 2 medium onions sliced
- ½ cup chopped cilantro
- 1 heaping teaspoon pureed ginger
- 1 heaping teaspoon pureed garlic
- 1 teaspoon cayenne pepper
- 1 heaping teaspoon ground coriander
- ½ teaspoon turmeric powder
- 1 teaspoon salt or to taste
- 6 tomatoes chopped
- 2 lbs lamb leg cut in 1" cubes with the bone
- 6 chicken thighs (with bone-in)

- 3-4 cups water
- A generous pinch of garam massala
- 2 Serrano chilies seeded and julienned

To Cook Daals:
- ½ cup channa daal
- ¼ cup masoor daal
- ¼ cup moong daal peeled (called *dhoolee moong*)
- ¼ cup moong daal whole unpeeled (called *sabat moong*)
- 1 teaspoon pureed ginger
- 1 teaspoon pureed garlic
- 1 teaspoon salt
- ¼ teaspoon turmeric
- ½ teaspoon ground coriander
- 3 cups water
- ¼ cup oil

Preparing the Cracked Wheat:
- 1 ½ cups cracked wheat
  (soaked in 2 cups water 4-6 hours or overnight)

To cook the meat:
Heat oil in a large heavy pan over a medium flame. Add cumin seeds and as soon as they begin to sizzle add the black cardamom, julienned ginger and two tablespoons of the chopped cilantro. Let the ginger and the cilantro sizzle for a few seconds. Add the sliced onion and sauté the onions stirring often. Sauté until most of the water from the onions has evaporated, and they start to turn an even very light golden brown.

Add the pureed ginger and garlic to the lightly browned onions. Sauté 15-20 seconds until the ginger and the garlic begin to lend their aroma to the mix. Add the cayenne pepper, coriander, turmeric and salt, and sauté the spices in the onion oil mix.

Add a few drops of water to the pot every 2-3 minutes as you sauté the spices. Repeat the process 3-4 times. Sautéing the spices is a crucial step in making any curry based dish to bring out all the flavors of the spices. At this stage add the chopped tomatoes and cook until the tomatoes begin to dissolve and break stir often as you cook the tomatoes. About 8-12 minutes.

(Close to being done, lentils will thicken up and begin to have a tendency to stick to the bottom of the pan. At this stage it is essential to stir often. Adjust the flame and water as needed to maintain the right consistency for the lentils to cook through until tender)

Add the lamb and chicken and sauté the meat in the onion and spice mixture, stirring occasionally. If the spice and meat mix seems to dry up too much as you sauté, add a few drops of water to retain moisture. Sauté for approximatley15-20 minutes. Next, add about 3 cups of water to the pot, cover and cook on a medium flame for 35-45 minutes.

To cook the lentils (daals):
In a separate pot, add all of the ingredients listed under 'to cook daals'. Cover the pot and let the lentils cook on a medium flame for 35-40 minutes. Stir often as you cook, and adjust the flame as needed. Try pressing a few grains of lentils between your fingers to test for doneness. Cook longer if needed, lentils should be soft and mash easily when pressed between fingers and thumb.

To cook the cracked wheat:
Boil wheat on a low flame with two cups of water for 25-30 minutes.

To finish the dish:
Carefully remove and discard all bones from the cooked meat. Puree the meat in a food processor in 2-3 batches; use ½ cup to 1 cup of water to empty the contents from the food processor. Puree half of the cooked lentils and combine the lentils and the cooked cracked wheat with the meat in a large pot. Slow cook the haleem on low heat covered for an hour to an hour and a half, stirring occasionally until most of the water has evaporated. The finished product will have a starchy batter like consistency. The cracked wheat will add volume to the dish.

(If possible, use a simmer plate for this last stage of slow cooking the haleem).

Add cilantro, green chopped chili pepper and garam massala.

Serve with a sautéed onion topping. Fresh julienned ginger, chopped cilantro, chopped Serrano chilies and lemon wedges on the side.

Tarka/Bhigar: or
sautéed onion topping:

- 1 onion thin sliced
- 1 cloves of garlic chopped
- 1 teaspoon chopped ginger
- ¼ teaspoon cumin seeds
- 2 tablespoons chopped cilantro
- ¼ cup oil

Heat oil in a frying pan. Brown the onions in the oil over a medium flame. Add the cumin seeds, ginger and garlic to the lightly browned onions and cook for another minute or so and pour the contents over the haleem.

Side garnishes for haleem:
- 2-4 lemons, each cut into four quarters
- 1 Serrano chili, finely chopped
- ¼ cup chopped cilantro
- ¼ cup ginger peeled and julienned

Serve the above ingredients on the side with haleem.

Serves 12-15

Neelo's Lamb Pot Roast

This recipe comes from one of my favorite cooking talent's in the family, my sister in law Neelo, who lives in Lahore, Pakistan. I have picked up many cooking tips and tricks from her over the years, and on many occasions I have enjoyed cooking together with her. Serve this roasted leg of lamb with deep fried potato wedges and other vegetables of your choice. It is great with rice or naan.

To marinate the leg of lamb
- ¼ cup lemon juice
- 1 teaspoon garlic Pureed
- 1 teaspoon crushed red Pepper
- ½ teaspoon cayenne Pepper
- 1 teaspoon garam massala (homemade or store bought)*
- 1 heaping teaspoon salt
- 1 cup yogurt
- 2-3 lb piece of leg of lamb

To cook the leg of lamb:
- ½ cup oil
- ½ teaspoon cumin seeds
- 1 black cardamom
- 5-6 black cloves
- 1 teaspoon whole black pepper corns
- 1 heaping teaspoon pureed ginger and garlic (see p. 217)
- 3-5 whole cloves garlic
- 2 ½ cups water

*See recipe homemade garam masala on page 215

Wash and pat dry the leg of lamb piece, and trim off all of the excess fat. Mix together in a mixing bowl the lemon juice, pureed garlic, crushed red pepper, the cayenne pepper, garam massala, salt and the yogurt.

With the tip of a sharp knife make several deep cuts on all sides of the meat, using your hands rub the meat all over with the prepared marinade and set aside to marinate for 2-4 hours. You can even let the meat marinate overnight.

In a heavy bottom pot, heat oil on medium flame, add cumin seeds to the hot oil. Let the cumin seeds sizzle in the oil for just a few seconds (5-10) and add the marinated lamb leg piece to the pot.

Cook the lamb on both sides in the hot oil, 5-7 minutes on each side; add the rest of the whole spices (black cardamom, black cloves and the black peppercorns), the pureed ginger and garlic and the garlic cloves.

Lower the heat, add water cover and continue to cook for an hour to an hour and a half, turning the meat a few times as you cook. Add more water and adjust the flame as needed. Insert the tip of a knife to test the meat for doneness meat should be tender and break away easy. If needed for added tenderness of meat, simmer using a simmer plate. Serve with the meat juices and spicy gravy that forms in the pot.

Garnish with deep fried potato wedges, tomatoes and chopped cilantro or mint leaves.
Serves 6-8

Kofta Curry

(Meatballs)

Please do not let the length of the recipe intimidate you from trying it. Read the recipe a few times and try to absorb each step as you envision it in your

mind's eye. You will realize it's pretty simple once you have gained some

familiarity with the steps involved.

Koftas simmering in a base sauce of onions, tomatoes and spices

For the Meatballs:

- 1 ½ to 2 lbs lean ground beef (15% fat) or
- 2 lbs ground chicken (use dark meat)
- ²/₃ cup finely chopped green onions
- 1 teaspoon pureed ginger
- 1 teaspoon pureed garlic
- ½ cup cilantro chopped (leaves and stems together)
- ¼ teaspoon crushed red pepper
- 2 Serrano green chilies seeded, washed and finely chopped
- 1 ½ teaspoon garam massala (store bought or homemade)*
- 1 teaspoon salt, or to taste
- 1 egg (use egg only if using ground beef- omit egg if using ground chicken)

- (a glass of cold water as an aid to form meatballs)
- 2 tablespoons oil for frying the meatballs

* See recipe for homemade garam massala on page 215

For the Sauce:

- ¹/₃ cup oil
- ¼ tea spoon cumin seeds

142

- 1 whole black cardamom, lightly pounded
- 1 teaspoon julienned ginger
- 2-4 tablespoons chopped cilantro
- 2 medium onions thin sliced
- 1 ½ teaspoon pureed ginger
- 1 ½ teaspoon pureed garlic
- Salt to taste
- $^1/_3$ teaspoon cayenne pepper
- ½ teaspoon crushed red pepper
- ¼ teaspoon turmeric powder
- ½ teaspoon ground cumin

- 1 teaspoon ground coriander
- 6-8 medium sized tomatoes seeded and chopped
- Garam massala for garnish
- 1 ½ cups water

Garnish:
- 1 Serrano chili
- 2-4 tablespoons cilantro
- 1 pinch of garam massala
- 6 boiled eggs, halved

To form meatballs:

In a large bowl with your hands combine the ground meat, green onions, ginger, garlic, cilantro, crushed red pepper, the chopped Serrano chilies, garam massala, salt and the (raw) egg and set aside.

Start with clean dry hands to form meatballs. Take a generous heaping tablespoon of the meat mixture and shape in the form of a ball. Dip fingers in cold water as an aid to form the meatballs. Place the formed meatballs in a tray or plate, and let the meatballs air dry for a few minutes.

For the curry sauce:

Heat oil in a cooking pot; add the cumin seeds, the black cardamom and cook for 10-15 seconds until the spices sizzle. Add the julienned ginger and about two tablespoons of the chopped cilantro. Sauté for another 10 seconds and add the sliced onions.

Sauté the onions, stirring often until they begin to change to a light golden brown color, and keep stirring to insure even browning-about 8-12 minutes. When the onions have browned to a light golden color, add the pureed ginger and garlic, stirring frequently for a couple of minutes. Add about ⅛ cup water to the pot. Add the salt, cayenne pepper, crushed red pepper, turmeric, ground cumin and the coriander to the pot.

Sauté the spices on medium heat and keep stirring for even cooking. Sprinkle with drops of water every few minutes to cool the contents in the pot and to keep the spice mixture from sticking to the bottom of the pan. Repeat this process for 8-10 minutes. As always this is a vital and a mandatory step in cooking a good curry sauce. **

Add the chopped tomatoes and cook for another 5-10 minutes. Transfer ¾ of the contents to a blender or food processor, and blend until smooth. Pour back in the pot, (using water as an aid to empty the contents from the blender). Add the remaining cilantro, cover and let slow cook for another 8-10 minutes.

To Saute the Meatballs:
- 2 tablespoons of oil
- In an open preferably non stick pan, add 2 tablespoons of the oil and layer the meatballs for a quick light browning on both sides. Sauté each side for just 1-3 minutes, drain on a plate lined with a double layer of paper towels.

Add the sautéed meatballs to the simmering tomato and spice curry sauce. Cover and let cook on medium low heat for about 15-20 minutes. Partially uncover and let simmer on slightly lower heat for another 10 minutes. For even cooking, stir the meatballs occasionally and gently as they simmer in the sauce.

Before serving, arrange boiled egg halves in between the meatballs for garnish.

Sprinkle chopped cilantro on top, and dust with a pinch of garam massala. Add the whole Serrano chili to the sauce for flavor.

Serve with rice, chappatis or naan.
Serves 8-10

**I demonstrate and stress this step strongly in my cooking classes, as it is an important step in cooking curry sauce based recipes in the Indian cuisine and important to employ for a good result.

Karahi Gosht

(Meat cooked in Wok)

Named after the pot it's cooked in, a *karahi* is an equivalent of a wok. Karahi gosht is a quick way to cook lamb, and offers another variation for cooking lamb curry. I usually cook this dish in two steps; first I will make the base curry sauce with tomato and spices in one pot then cook the meat in a separate pot with some pureed ginger, garlic and spices. Next I fold the sautéed meat into the curry sauce and simmer the meat in the sauce on low flame for a few minutes (25-30) to complete the dish.

For the Sauce
- ¼ cup oil
- ⅛ teaspoon cumin seeds
- 1 teaspoon julienned ginger
- ½ cup chopped cilantro
- 1 ½ heaping teaspoon pureed ginger
- 1 ½ heaping teaspoon pureed garlic
- 1 teaspoon salt
- ½ teaspoon ground red pepper (cayenne pepper)
- 8 medium sized tomatoes chopped

Some water as cooking aid

For the Meat:
- 2 lbs leg of lamb cut up into one inch cubes, (cut with the bone)
- 2 tablespoons oil
- 1 heaping teaspoon pureed ginger
- 1 heaping teaspoon pureed garlic
- 2 tablespoons chopped cilantro
- 1/8 teaspoon ground turmeric
- 1 teaspoon crushed red pepper
- ½ teaspoon cayenne pepper
- ½ teaspoon salt

- ½ cup water

To Finish:
- 2 tablespoons dried fenugreek leaves or *Methi*
  (available at the Indian/Pakistani spice stores under the label 'Kasoori Methi')
- 1 Serrano chili thin sliced and seeded

For the Base curry Sauce

Heat oil in a wok or a deep pan, add a pinch of cumin seeds to the oil as it warms up. Add julienned ginger and half of the cilantro, quick stir in hot oil for a few seconds.

Add pureed ginger and garlic to the hot oil mixture and stir for a minute. Now add the salt, crushed red pepper, the cayenne pepper and stir for a couple of minutes. Sprinkle a tablespoon of water if the mixture becomes too dry, and continue to sauté the spices for another minute or two.

Add the chopped tomatoes and cook on a medium high flame uncovered for 5-7 minutes, cover and continue cook on a slightly lower flame, 7-10 minutes. Stir often to keep mixture from sticking to the bottom of the pan and to ensure even cooking of the tomato and spice mix.

To sauté meat:

Season the meat with the pureed ginger and garlic. Add the salt, crushed red pepper, turmeric and the chopped cilantro. Heat oil in a deep frying pan or a wok, add the seasoned meat, sauté and sear quickly on a high flame for 5-7 minutes. Lower the flame and add water. Continue to cook on a low flame for 25-35 minutes, adding more water if necessary until the meat is cooked through and tender.

Stir often as you cook.

Fold the cooked meat into the prepared base sauce and simmer on low for 20-25 minutes, stirring often. The dish is cooked when the oil in the pan starts to surface at the sides of the pan and the meat is tender and breaks easy. Add dried fenugreek (methi) leaves and the sliced Serrano chili. Cover and let sit for a few minutes before serving.

Serve with rice or naan.

Serves 4-6

Apa's Amb Kalia

(Sweet and Sour Mango Curry)

One of Apa's (my late mother) best recipes.

The natural season for this dish is from late spring thru mid summer, as the main ingredient for this recipe, "raw mangoes" are available in the Indian sub-continent usually during these months. At Indian grocery markets in California I've seen them over a longer stretch. This dish is best served with tandoori naans or tandoori parathas, although regular pita bread could be a substitute bread or even better, homemade parathas (see recipe for parathas under Indian/Pakistani flat breads).

To boil the raw Mango:
- 2 medium sized raw mangoes, peeled and cut in wedges with a sharp knife
  (discard the inner white raw pit, keeping the hardened shell intact with the flesh)
- 1 teaspoon turmeric
- 1 teaspoon Salt
- 4-6 cups of water

Boil mango wedges in water with salt and turmeric, for about 10 minutes, drain the wedges in a colander and set aside.

For the Lamb Curry:
- ½ cup oil
- 1 black cardamom
- 2 medium onions, peeled and thinly slices
- 1 teaspoon pureed ginger
- 1 teaspoon pureed garlic
- 4 medium tomatoes chopped
- Salt to taste
- ½ tea spoon ground cayenne pepper
- 1 ½-2lbs. Lamb shanks cut in 2" pieces

(or same portion leg of lamb cut up in 2" pieces)
- ¼ cup slivered almonds
- 5-7 green cardamoms
- 1 ½ cup water
- 1½ cup sugar
- Some additional water on the side as a cooking aid

Heat oil in a cooking pot over a medium flame. Add black cardamom and let sizzle in hot oil for 3-5 seconds. Add the sliced onions and sauté until a light golden color, about 15-20 minutes. Stir often for even browning.

Add the ginger and garlic, sauté for 1 minute, stir often. Next add the salt and cayenne pepper and sauté the spices for 2-5 minutes. Stir and add a few drops of water as you sauté to keep the spices from sticking to the bottom of the pan. Add the chopped tomatoes. Cook the tomatoes for 7-12 minutes, as the tomatoes dissolve in the pan; break them up with the stirring spoon.

Add the meat to the pot, sear the meat in the tomato, onion and spice mixture. Stir often as you continue to sear the meat in the curry sauce for 12-15 minutes. Reduce heat if needed. Add the green cardamoms and almonds to the pot.

Add water and let the meat simmer on a low flame for 20-25 minutes. (Eyeball the cooking meat to make sure there is enough liquid in the pot. It should have a rich sauce, if the sauce around the meat appears too dry, add a few tablespoons of additional water-¼ cup or more).

When the meat is almost done add the partially cooked mango wedges and sugar. Cover and simmer, do not let the sauce caramelize, stir occasionally. Use a simmer plate for extra care.

The sauce should be rich and not too runny

Serve with tandoori naans or parathas.

Serves 8-10

Fish
Recipes

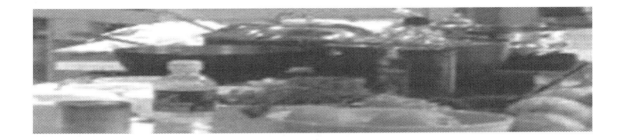

I am sharing with you here a just a few simple and quick recipes some of these
of course I grew up with and then started cooking for my family and friends,
and some of these recipes I picked up and developed over the years

Dahee Walee Machee

Apa's Version (Fish Cooked in Yogurt)

"Eat carefully and watch for any spike or bone before each morsel!" was the word of caution from Apa (our mother) each time 'Dahee Walee Machlee' was on the dinner menu. This has been one of my favorite dishes from a very young age, and is one of the most delicious ways to enjoy fish.

- 2 medium onions, peeled and thin sliced
- ½ tea spoon cumin seeds
- 6 medium tomatoes, pureed through a food processor
- 2 lbs halibut, cod or grouper, cut into large squares
- 2 tablespoons pureed ginger
- ½ tea spoon ground Cayenne pepper
- 1 teaspoon Garam Massala
- salt to taste
- 1 cup yogurt (mixed with a spoon to smooth out any lumps)
- ¼ cup Olive or Vegetable Oil

Brown onions in oil with the cumin seeds on a medium flame, until, it turns a light golden color. Stir occasionally to ensure even browning of sliced onion. At this stage add the pureed ginger, sauté the ginger for a few seconds, stirring constantly. Now add the dry spices salt and pepper and sauté for a couple of minutes, adding drops of water if needed to keep the ingredients from sticking to the bottom of the pan and/or burning.

Add the pureed tomatoes and the garam massala and continue to cook for 15 to 20 minutes for the tomatoes to cook through, stirring occasionally. Do not let the sauce reduce too much and if it has add ½ a cup of water to adjust consistency of the curry sauce. Layer the fish squares on top of the curry sauce in the cooking pot and top with yogurt, cook on a low flame, covered for 20-25 minutes. Sauce in the cooked dish should be the consistency of a thick spaghetti sauce, if it appears too runny, finish cooking on a low flame still, but with the pot partially covered.

Serve with plain boiled, preferably 'Basmati' rice and enjoy!
Serves: 6-8

Fish Baked in Green Herbs

Halibut is a great pick for this recipe, easy to fix, serve with a side of vegetables and rice.

Step1:
- ½ teaspoon cumin seeds
- 1 teaspoon turmeric powder
- 2 heaping tablespoons garlic pureed
- 2 green chilies seeded and chopped
- 1 teaspoon freshly grated lemon peel
- salt to taste
  (puree all of the above ingredients in a mini chopper, food processor or a blender)

- ¼ cup extra virgin olive oil, or any vegetable oil
- ½ teaspoon crushed red pepper

Step 2:
- 1 cup Yogurt
- 1 cup chopped cilantro
  (Both ingredients blended smooth together in a food processor or blender)
- ¼ cup finely chopped green onion

Step3:
- 2-3 lbs Halibut filets
- A pinch of salt
- ¼ teaspoon freshly ground black pepper

Wash halibut filets and pat dry using paper towels. Give the filets a light dusting of salt and freshly ground black pepper and set aside for use later.

Step 1:

Heat oil in a cooking pan; add the pureed ingredients of step 1 to the heated oil and sauté on medium flame for 15 to 18 minutes, until all of the spices are cooked through. Add the crushed red pepper. Keep stirring and give it a light sprinkle of water as you continue to cook, to keep the spice mixture (a.k.a. 'massala') from drying up too much or sticking to the bottom of the pan.

Step2:

Add the yogurt and cilantro mixture to the *massala* in the cooking pot, and cook until the mixture comes to a boil. Add the chopped green onions and let boil for a couple of minutes.

Step3:

In the meantime arrange halibut filets in a deep baking dish and pour the sautéed spice (massala) mixture over the fish, bake for 40 minutes, uncovered at 350 degrees.

Serves 8-10

Cooking Rice
The Indian Style

Rice is a staple with an Indian/ Pakistani meal. With basmati rice being the most favored variety. Basmati rice is grown in the Northern part of India, and in parts of Pakistan closer to India, mainly in Punjab. It is preferred for its distinct characteristics of aroma and the size of the grain. When cooked each grain of the rice stands separate. The soil and the climate of the region lend this rice its unique characteristics and make it hard to duplicate in any other part of the world.

To get the optimum results from the recipes in this section using 'basmati' rice is a <u>must</u>. It is available at most Indian/Pakistani grocery stores, ethnic markets, and these days you will see many regular super markets carry sacks of basmati rice as well. All imported from India and Pakistan.

Just like it's advised for wine, basmati rice is improved when allowed to age. I remember growing up in Lahore (Pakistan), we would always have loads of basmati rice stored in the pantry of our kitchen, placed there to age. The portion being utilized for daily cooking would be the portion that had been allowed to *sit* in the storeroom for months before being put to use.

They say that the process of aging enhances the natural characteristics of basmati rice, both in the size of the grain and its aroma. The seasonal changes also have an enriching impact on the *sitting* rice, especially when allowed to rest through a season of monsoon and/or winter rains.

Boiled Basmati Rice with Green Peas and Whole Spices

Though it's not uncommon to have plain boiled rice with an Indian meal, I rarely leave rice just plain in my cooking. If nothing else, I'll add some salt, cumin seeds and some additional whole spices and on occasions a vegetable (peas being the most commonly used in rice) or two.

- 2 cups (basmati) rice, washed
- 4 to 6 cups water
- 1 teaspoon salt
- ½ teaspoon cumin seeds
- ½ stick of cinnamon
- 1 black cardamom (optional, if available)
- 2 tablespoons oil
- 2 cups peas
- 2 tablespoons chopped cilantro (optional if available)

Boil rice in an uncovered pot with salt, cumin seeds, cinnamon stick and the whole black cardamom for 7-10 minutes, until partially done.

Reduce heat, test for partial doneness by pressing a few grains of rice between your fingers, it should be slightly tender at the ends and still have some firmness in the middle as you press on the grain.

Drain rice and transfer it back to the pot, return the pot to the stove and set it on low heat. Fold in the oil and the peas, cover and continue steaming on a very low flame for about 10-12 minutes until done. Turn off heat; keep rice covered until ready to serve.

Garnish with chopped cilantro before serving.

Plain rice works well with any Indian curry, especially great with daal, spinach and fish recipes.

Serves 6-8

Vegetable Rice Biryani

Here is my vegetarian version of the traditional biryani. It's packed with flavors, vegetables and nuts, great for entertaining or for any special meal.

To boil rice:
- 2 ½ cups rice (basmati rice)
- ½ cup chopped mint
- ½ cup chopped cilantro
- 1 Serrano chili chopped
- 1 teaspoon pureed garlic
- 1 teaspoon salt
- ½ teaspoon cumin seed
- ½ teaspoon ground turmeric
- 8-10 cups water

For the mixed vegetable layer of biryani:
- ¼ cup oil
- 1 teaspoon cumin seeds
- 1 teaspoon black cloves
- 1/2 teaspoon black peppercorns
- 1" stick cinnamon
- 1 black cardamom
- 1 medium onion chopped
- 1 teaspoon pureed ginger
- 1 teaspoon pureed garlic
- Salt to taste
- ¼ teaspoon crushed red pepper
- 2 cups frozen mixed vegetables
- ½ teaspoon saffron threads soaked in ¼ cup milk or water

For Garnish:

- ¼ cup oil
- 2 medium onions sliced
- A pinch of cumin seeds
- ¼ cup raw cashews
- ¼ cup slivered almonds
- ¼ cup golden raisins

To boil rice:

Start with boiling water with herbs and spices listed, when the water comes to a boil add the rice and boil to a partial tender stage (10-12 minutes). To determine that par boiled stage spoon some boiling rice out of the pot and feel it between your fingers. If the rice breaks easy at ends and is still a little firm in the middle the rice has reached the par boiled stage. Drain the rice in a colander.

For the vegetables:

Heat oil in a deep pot or a frying pan over a medium flame. Add the cumin seeds, cloves, black peppercorns, stick cinnamon and the black cardamom to the hot oil and let the spices sauté for a few seconds. Next add the chopped onion and sauté until the onion starts to look translucent and begins to turn a light golden color at the edges, about 7-10 minutes.

Add the pureed ginger and garlic, sauté stirring often until the ginger and garlic begin to lend out their aroma, 15-20 seconds. At this point add the salt, the crushed red pepper and the mixed vegetables. Cook for about 7-8 minutes and remove pan from the stove.

To assemble the rice and vegetables: Pre-heat oven to 225°-250°
In a deep serving dish or a cooking pot layer half of the rice and top with the cooked vegetables. Cover with the remaining rice, drizzle the soaked saffron with the soaking liquid over the rice. Cover tightly with foil or pot cover and bake in the pre-heated oven for about 20-30 minutes.

To prepare the garnish:
Heat oil in a deep frying pan add the sliced onions and the cumin seeds, let the onions sauté lightly for an even golden brown color, stirring often as you sauté. When the onions are evenly browned add the nuts and sauté them for a few seconds, add the raisins as you continue to sauté for a few seconds more, about 8-10 seconds.

Spread prepared garnish over rice before serving.

Serves 8-10

Chicken Biryani

A Pakistani/Indian rice dish cooked generally with meat, and could by itself be a complete meal. In this simplified version of this very popular dish I cook it with boneless chicken breast, and of course always with 'basmati' rice please.

Note:
This dish involves three cooking steps:
   a)   the first step is to prepare a curry base for the dish,
   b)   the second step includes partially boiling the rice with herbs and whole spices and
   c)   the third step consists of first assembling and then baking the curry base and the rice together to complete the dish

The Curry Base:

Ingredients:
(for the first step)

Biryani prep at the cooking school

- ¼ cup cooking oil
- ½ teaspoon cumin seeds
- 1 teaspoon whole black peppercorns
- 1 black cardamom (if available)
- 1 teaspoon black cloves
- ½ inch piece of stick cinnamon
- 1 large onion peeled and thin sliced
- 1 slightly heaping teaspoon pureed ginger
- 1 slightly heaping teaspoon pureed garlic
- 1 teaspoon salt or to taste
- ½ teaspoon ground red pepper
- ¼ teaspoon turmeric powder
- 1 teaspoon ground coriander

- ¼ cup full cream yogurt
- 1 ½ half pounds to 2 pounds boneless chicken breast, cut into 2" cubes
- 5-6 green cardamoms slightly pounded to crack open
- A pinch of saffron threads soaked in 2 to 3 tablespoons of warm milk
- Water as cooking aid

Heat oil in a cooking pot over a medium flame. Add the cumin seeds, peppercorns, black cardamom, black cloves, cinnamon stick and the sliced onions, sauté the onions to a light golden brown stirring often for even light browning.

Add the pureed ginger and garlic and sauté for another two to three minutes, as you stir often; as the ginger and garlic begin to lend their flavor to the oil add the salt, the red pepper, turmeric and coriander.

Cook the spice mixture on a medium flame, stir frequently, add a few drops of water every 3-4 minutes to keep the spices from overcooking or sticking to the bottom of the pan. Repeat these steps two to three times.

Add the blended yogurt to the pot, smooth the yogurt into the sauce with a spoon, cook for 5-6 minutes. Add the cubed chicken and sauté the meat in the spice mixture (or the 'massala' as it is referred to in an Indian or a Pakistani kitchen).

Continue to cook the meat in the massala (spice mixture), stirring to coat all pieces well. Cook for about 10-12 minutes, add ¼ cup water, cover and cook on medium flame for another 10-15 minutes so the chicken is cooked through. The chicken mixture should have a moderate amount of thick soup like massala sauce around it. (If the sauce in the pot seems too thick, add 2-4 tablespoons of water to dilute the sauce).

Step Two, Partially Boiling the Rice in Herbs:

- 2 cups *basmati* rice

- 1 Serrano (green) chili seeded and chopped
- 1 bunch green onion chopped
- 2 tablespoons chopped mint leaves
- ¼ cup chopped cilantro
- 1 teaspoon salt
- 6-8 cups of water
- A few drops of lemon yellow food color

Partially boil rice in a large pot in about 8 cups of water, the serrano chili, green onion, mint leaves, cilantro and salt (10-12 minutes). Test for partial doneness by feeling a few grains of rice between your fingers. If the rice breaks easy at ends and is a little firm in the middle, the rice has reached the par boiled stage.

Drain the rice in a colander and keep aside until ready for the next step. Pour a few drops of lemon yellow food color over the par boiled rice and fold the rice gently with a spoon, so the rice has a dual shade of white and yellow.

Layering the chicken and the rice and completing the Cooking:
In a deep pot, layer half of the rice at the bottom of the pan, cover with the chicken mixture and add 5-6 green cardamoms to the chicken mixture. Top with the remaining rice, pour the milk soaked saffron threads on top, cover and bake in a 225° oven for about 25 minutes.

To Serve:
Gently fold the chicken and the rice together, transfer to a serving platter and top with the prepared topping of fried onions and raisins. Serve with yogurt and/or your favorite curry dish.

Biryani Topping:

- 1 medium onion thin sliced
- ¼ cup raisins
- ¼ cup raw cashews
- ¼ cup oil
- a pinch of cumin seeds

Heat oil in a deep frying pan. Brown onions lightly in hot oil, stir as you sauté for an even brown, add raisins, cashews and cumin seeds and fry for another minute or so. With a slotted spoon, pick up the sautéed onions, cashews and raisins. Spread over the rice and serve.

Serves 8-10

Mattar Palao

This rice dish can be made with vegetables or garbanzo beans. I make it most often with peas; you can also use other combinations of frozen vegetables or garbanzo beans. The rest of the ingredients and the steps remain the same. For a richer version you can substitute chicken stock for water.

- ¼ cup olive oil
- ½ teaspoon cumin seeds
- 1 stick cinnamon
- 1/2 teaspoon black peppercorns
- 1 black cardamom (slightly cracked open)
- 1 medium onion thin sliced
- 1 teaspoon pureed garlic
- 1 teaspoon salt
- 2 cups frozen peas or (one 16 oz can garbanzo beans, drained and washed)
- 2 cups *basmati* rice, washed and soaked in water for 10 minutes and drained
- 3 cups water or chicken stock*

Heat oil in a deep cooking pot, add cumin seeds, stick cinnamon, black peppercorns and the black cardamom and sauté spices for 15 to 20 seconds, as the spices begin to sizzle add the sliced onions.

Cook on medium low heat stirring often for even browning. When the onions turn a light golden color add pureed garlic, salt and the frozen peas (or the garbanzo beans, if using garbanzo beans instead of peas).

Stir for a couple of minutes, add the measured rice. Sauté the mixture for 3 to 5 minutes, add the chicken stock or water, liquid should be enough to barely cover the rice surface. Cover and cook for 10 to 12 minutes on a medium high flame, once the liquid starts to boil set the pot with the cover on into a 250° preheated oven for about 20 minutes, lower the oven to 200 ° and bake rice for another 10-15 minutes. Remove from oven and keep covered until ready to serve. Rice pot can be kept in oven set to warm until ready to serve. Sprinkle with additional cumin seeds if desired.

Serves 8

*I prefer to use homemade chicken stock. Following is recipe for homemade chicken stock:

Homemade chicken stock:

- 2 chicken legs or thighs
- 2 cloves of garlic
- 1 teaspoon salt
- ¼ teaspoon black pepper corns
- 6-8 black cloves
- 1 black cardamom
- ½ a stick of cinnamon
- 4 cups water

Add all the ingredients listed above in a deep pot, cook over medium high heat. Boil for 20-25 minutes, reduce flame, cover the pot and simmer for another 20 minutes. Strain into a container and reserve for use. Chicken stock can be frozen for use later. Freeze in an airtight container with a tight lid.

Festive 3 color Rice

This is just a fun way to present plain boiled rice. Involves a few steps, but if you are having a couple of friends over for dinner and wish to present rice with a little twist and variation this is a good recipe to go with. I usually serve it in a white platter and show off the three variations of color in small portions on the same platter.

- 2 cups basmati rice washed
- 2-3 small pieces stick cinnamon
- ¼ teaspoon cumin seeds
- 1 black cardamom
- 1 teaspoon salt
- 2 tablespoons oil
- 3 cups water

Heat oil in a heavy bottom pan, add cumin seeds, stick cinnamon and the black cardamom. Sauté for about one minute, add salt and then the rice. Stir to mix well, add the measured water. Cover and cook on medium flame for about 10-12 minutes, reduce flame and let the rice steam until done, about 8-10 minutes. Turn off flame and keep the pot covered.

Divide the cook rice is three equal portions.

For the plain white rice:
- 3 tablespoons chopped onions
- 1 tablespoon oil
- ⅓ of the cooked rice

In a deep bowl add oil and onions and the rice, fold all ingredients together gently. And reserve in the mixing bowl.

For the green rice:
- 3 tablespoons chopped green or regular onions
- ¼ cup chopped fresh dill or dried dill
- 1 tablespoon oil
- ¹/₃ of the cooked rice

In a mixing bowl mix the herbs and the oil, and fold in the rice gently. Set aside until ready to serve.

For the yellow rice:
- 2 tablespoons chopped green bell pepper
- 2 tablespoons chopped red bell pepper
- 2 tablespoons chopped yellow bell pepper
- 2 tablespoons chopped cilantro
- 2 tablespoons chopped green onion
- 2 tablespoons oil
- A few drops yellow food color
- ¹/₃ of the cooked rice

In a deep bowl mix together the bell peppers, chopped cilantro, green onion and the oil.

In a separate bowl add rice and pour food color on the rice. Gently fold rice to mix in the food color. Add bell pepper and herb mix to the rice and fold in to mix well. Set aside until ready to serve.

Serving the Rice:

In a serving platter arrange the yellow, white and the green rice alternatively in three separate portions and serve.

Serves 4-6

Murgh Palao (Chicken Pala-o)

Basmati rice cooked with chicken

My version for chicken palao is quick, made with boneless chicken, whole spices, ginger and garlic. Great with curry dishes, plain yogurt or can be enjoyed just by itself. Chicken palao with shammi kabobs* is another favored combination, and one of my favorite ways to enjoy the two dishes together.

*see recipe for shammi kabobs under appetizers

- ¼ cup oil
- ½ teaspoon cumin seeds
- 1 teaspoon black pepper corns
- ¼ teaspoon cloves
- 1 black cardamom
- 1 stick cinnamon
- 1 medium onion sliced
- 1 teaspoon pureed ginger
- 1 teaspoon pureed garlic
- 1 teaspoon salt
- 1 ½ lbs boneless chicken, cut up in small 1" cubes
- 3 cups water
- 2 cups basmati rice, washed and drained

Pre heat the oven at 250°
Heat oil in a cooking pot, add the cumin seeds, pepper corns, cloves, black cardamom and the cinnamon stick and let whole spices sizzle in the hot oil for a few seconds, until they start to lend their aroma to the oil. (10-15 seconds)

Add the sliced onion and sauté until the water from the onions has dried up and they start to turn a light golden color. Stir often for even browning. As the onion begins to turn a light golden color, add the pureed ginger and the garlic, sauté for a few seconds and add salt.

Add the cubed chicken. Cook for 12-15 minutes, until the chicken has cooked through and lightly browned on all sides, stir often as you sauté the chicken. Add water, cover the pot and let the chicken cook for 10-15 minutes to form a stock. Uncover and add rice, stir to mix in the rice. Cover and cook on a medium flame until the liquid starts to boil.

Transfer the covered pot to the preheated oven and finish cooking in the oven, about 20-25 minutes. Keep covered until ready to serve.

Serves 6-8

Flat Breads
And Naans

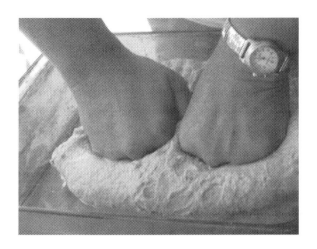

Traditionally speaking, breads typically cooked within majority of the Indian/Pakistani homes on a daily basis are the flat breads, for example the chappatis, parathas, and on occasions the deep fried poori.

Other breads including different varieties of naans, kulcha, taftana, tandoori roti and tandoori paratha etc. are mostly prepared by and sold at local restaurants and tandoors, fondly also referred to as 'dhabas'. And are typically ordered out.

The selection you will see in this section includes recipes for breads that are commonly prepared in home kitchens.

Chappati

Imagine the luxury of sitting at the dinner table and someone in the kitchen whipping up <u>fresh</u> piping hot chappatis one at a time for your culinary pleasures. This is the traditional luxury of practice enjoyed by some in India and Pakistan. And now fortunately for us right here in the U.S. we are offered the same indulgence at the local Indian/Pakistani cafes, especially in larger cities. Here is recipe for whenever you feel like treating yourself to a fresh cooked chappati right in your own kitchen.

- 4 cups chappati flour (or 'atta' available at Indian/Pakistani grocery stores)
- 1 teaspoon salt
- 2 cups water (plus another two cups set aside for additional amounts as needed)
- 4 tablespoons oil (optional)
- ¼ teaspoon ajwain seeds (optional)
- ½ teaspoon cumin seeds (optional)

Mixing and kneading by hand:
In a large deep platter or dish add all the dry ingredients, mix in the oil and slowly start adding water. Start by adding one cup of water at a time, and with your hands start bringing the mixture together until a coarse meal forms. Gently fold together to form a large dough ball.

Gradually add more water in controlled amounts (a tablespoon or two at a time) to moisten any and all remaining flour that is still dry around the edges and bring together to combine into the larger portion.

Knead the dough with the knuckles of your tightly fisted hands; dipping your hands in a bowl of water periodically as you knead, this helps ease the kneading process. The dough should neither be too sticky or too stiff. If it is stiff add a little water. If it is too sticky add some extra flour. Knead until it feels a little elastic, 4-6 minutes.

Form a large patty and give it a light sprinkle of a few drops of water, cover with plastic and let it sit for a few minutes before beginning to form smaller dough balls to make chappatis or parathas.

Preparing the flour mix using the food processor:

Mix the salt, flour, ajwain and cumin seeds in a bowl. Transfer contents to the container of a food processor; add oil and one cup of water as you start to mix on low speed. Eyeball the mix and with the processor on, gradually add more water if mix appears dry, the dough will gather and form a dough ball, mix for about one minute. Transfer the dough ball to a pan and knead with your hands for 2-4 minutes. Form a large patty, sprinkle with a few drops of water, cover the pan with plastic wrap and set aside for 15 minutes before using.

Again, add more flour if the dough is too sticky and more water if it is too stiff as you knead.

Forming Chappatis:

Take a small portion of dough, and form a small ball. Use dry flour as aid in forming the dough ball. Continue making dough balls and place them in a platter covered with plastic wrap or a moist towel until ready to use. In the meantime pre-heat a large frying pan or a flat pan over the stove, set on medium heat. The traditional pan to make a chappati is called a 'tava' and you can usually find one at an Indian spice store. I have also bought tortilla makers from kitchen equipment stores and they work just as well.

Take a dough ball and roll it out on a flat surface with a rolling pin aided with dry flour, shape it round like a tortilla. Turn over and roll out the flip side, finish flattening the chappati by tossing it lightly between the palms of your hands if needed. Spread the flattened chappati on the heated pan, cook for a few seconds on one side, turn over to cook on the other side. Repeat turning the chappati a couple of times or as needed to ensure even cooking on both sides. Serve warm with meat and vegetable dishes.

Makes 8-10 chappatis

CAUTION: Regulating the proper temperature of the pan is a crucial step in cooking chappatis. If the pan is too hot the chappati will turn yellow and start to burn as soon as it is spread on the hot pan, if the pan is not hot enough it will stick to the pan. Adjust heat as needed.

Any left over dough can be stored in an airtight container in the refrigerator for 2-3 days.

Plain Paratha

A paratha is flat bread cooked in butter or oil. Traditionally it is served for breakfast with omelets, but it can be served with any meal. The paratha dough ball is flattened slightly, brushed with oil or butter, rolled up and then twisted and curled into a flat patty. The curled up patty is then spread with a rolling pin to flatten as a tortilla and cooked on a hot griddle called 'tava', it can also be cook using a frying pan. The rolling and curling of the dough is what creates the layers in the paratha. Just like the croissant these layers are characteristic of the paratha. It is brushed with oil as it is being cooked. If it wasn't the fear of calories it would be a part of my meals on a daily basis, but occasionally it's a lovely treat for a Sunday brunch.

Prepare dough following the dough recipe for chappati.

Keep dough balls covered with plastic until ready to use

For forming paratha:

- ½ stick melted butter or
- ½ cup oil

Divide prepared dough into 8-10 equal portions, take each piece and with the aid of dry flour form a dough ball. Place prepared dough balls in a pan and cover with plastic.

Pre-heat a large frying pan over medium heat.

(The traditional pan to make Indian/Pakistani flat breads is called a 'tava' and you can usually find one at an Indian spice store, tortilla makers available at kitchen equipment stores can be used as well).

178

Brush the top with oil or melted butter (Fig 1)

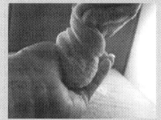

Roll up the buttered dough (fig 2)

Twist and curl as you press down the rolled dough (fig 3)

Place the curled up disc on a flat surface (fig 4)

Flatten with a rolling pin (fig 5)

Take a dough ball; place on a flat surface lightly dusted with flour, using a rolling pin spread it in the shape of a small circle approximately 3 inches in diameter. Brush top of the spread piece with butter or oil (fig 1), starting at the end away from you roll up the flattened dough towards you (fig 2).

Hold the rolled dough in one hand and form a disc by twisting and curling as you press the rolled dough down in the palm of your other hand (fig 3). Place the curled up disc on a flat surface (fig 4), with a rolling pin spread and shape it round like a tortilla (fig 5), flip sides and continue spreading. Pick up the flattened piece and finish spreading by tossing between the palms of your hands. Spread gently on the heated pan, cook for a minute on one side, turn over to cook on the other side. Brush each side lightly with oil or butter as you cook the *paratha*. Repeat turning the paratha as needed to ensure even cooking on both sides. Cook on a moderately hot pan or griddle. Serve warm with meat and vegetable dishes.
Makes 8-10 parathas

CAUTION: Regulating the proper temperature of the pan is crucial in cooking any flat bread. If the pan is too hot the paratha will start to burn as soon as it is spread on the hot pan, if the pan is not hot enough the dough will start to stick to the pan. Adjust heat as needed.

Make sure the flat bread is cooked even inside and out, cook to a light golden color on both sides.

Roghani Naan

The 'Roghani /or Tandoori Naan' is typically cooked inside an Indian Tandoori Oven, since most homes are not equipped with the *Tandoor*, this version is designed to cook this traditional Indian/Pakistani flat bread on the grill.

- 4 cups all purpose flour
- 1 seven gram packet instant yeast
- 2 teaspoons salt
- 3 teaspoons sugar
- 2 teaspoons baking soda
- 1 cup whole milk
- ½ cup oil
- ½ to ¾ cups water
- 1 cup dry flour as an aid to forming naans

Mix all of the dry ingredients in a deep bowl, add milk and oil and mix well. Gradually start adding water, 3-4 tablespoons at a time and mix and gather dough as you start kneading it with your hands. Continue kneading for about 7-10 minutes. Gather dough to form a huge ball, sprinkle water on top, cover with plastic wrap and let sit at room temperature for about an hour before using to make naans.

Divide dough into 6 equal parts, and aided with dry flour form dough balls. Start placing the dough balls on a plate or a cookie sheet. Cover with plastic wrap and let sit at room temperature until ready to use.

Preheat outdoor grill on high for 10 minutes, keep covered. Then reduce all burners to medium. Heat a pizza stone on top of the grill, cover the grill and let the stone preheat for a few minutes.(I have on occasion used a heavy limestone tile in the same way. But a good quality strong and well made pizza stone is a better option, sold at many gourmet food stores)

Take a dough ball and place it on a flat surface dusted with dry flour.
Using the tips of your fingers, aided by dry flour flatten the dough ball to form a round about 8-10 inches in diameter. Finish spreading by flipping the flattened dough a few times between the palms of your hands. Spread the flattened piece on the heated tile and let cook for a few minutes (3-5 minutes, please know that the cooking time will vary based on the temperature of your grill). Cover the grill and check every two to three minutes for doneness. Flip sides if needed to brown the top side. You can also finish cooking in a preheated oven (350°) for 2-3 minutes.
Brush lightly with oil and serve.

Serves 6

Indian/Pakistani Desserts

Ahh . . . *desserts!* -Oh yes, now we are talking . . . fixing and enjoying desserts both happen to be a passion of mine, making desserts is what really got me interested in cooking in the first place. And for me it is these masterful European, French, Italian and American desserts. Every time I prepare a dessert, to me it is like painting a picture, sketching a piece of art, putting some color in it, dressing it up right for the occasion and you are all set to have a party.

Zarda
(sweet rice)

The attraction for these European pastries is not too far fetched for an Indian or a Pakistani, as we grow up loving and enjoying European desserts, a taste and a palate left behind by many invaders that touched that land. Hey, we are no dummies-we kept the good stuff . . . and the rest, as they say, is 'history'. In this section I am including mostly traditional desserts of the Indo/ Pak sub-continent and a couple of 'European' desserts that have made their way into the Indian/Pakistani cuisine and have a slight Indian twist to them.

Gajjar (Carrot) Halwa

As far as I am concerned, this is the ultimate dessert. Consumed mainly in the winter months this is a dessert fit for royalty. My version below is quick to cook, and comes out just as delicious and flavorful as some of the more traditional recipes that start with boiling the carrots in a ton of milk . . . or almost a ton! Taste wise, it offers all the flavors the traditional recipe does.

- ¼ cup oil
- 1 stick butter
- 6-8 green cardamoms, pounded
- ½ cup slivered almonds
- 10 medium carrots
  (Peeled and grated or coarsely chopped in a food processor)
- 1 cup powdered milk
- 1 cup ricotta cheese
- 1 cup half and half
- 1 cup sugar
- A pinch of saffron threads soaked in ¼ cup half and half
- A pinch of salt
- ¼ cup chopped pistachios

Heat oil in a deep pan, as the oil heats up add butter. Start to melt the butter, add the cardamoms and almonds to the melting butter and sauté for a few seconds. Keep constant eyes on the pot making sure not to let the almonds brown too much. Stir often as you sauté the almonds, as soon as they start to change color at the edges add the carrots and cook the carrots in the butter almond mixture for about 25 minutes, stirring frequently.

Add in the dry milk, ricotta cheese and the half and half. Reduce the heat and continue cooking stirring as you continue to cook. Add the soaked saffron. Continue cooking the mix on a medium low flame for 25-45 minutes, stirring often as you slow cook.

Add sugar and the pinch of salt, and continue to cook on a medium low flame. This dessert dish requires a lot of slow cooking and frequent stirring toward the end, and is best simmered by giving it some indirect source of heat. I usually create that indirect source of heat by using a simmer plate between the pan and the flame. Slow simmer on a very low flame for another 30-40 minutes or as needed. When the melted butter starts to surface around the edges turn off the flame, and let the dish sit. Garnish with pistachios before serving

Preferably prepare it a day before serving for all the flavors to be absorbed well.

Gajjar (carrot) Halwa stores for days in the refrigerator and for several weeks in the freezer. Stored halwa can be micro waved before serving.

Adjust the amount of sugar to taste.

Serves 8-12

Sooji Halwa

They say that you've not celebrated '*eid*' until you've had <u>sooji halwa</u>. Though a must have for eid (a Muslim religious celebration), sooji halwa is enjoyed year round as a favored brunch item for Sunday mornings, with pooris and a side savory dish like channa. It's also works as a perfect dessert when served after dinner. In India and Pakistan halwa/poori/channa breakfast is sold at side walk cafes and sweet shops around town, often picked up and brought to be enjoyed at home. However, when it comes to halwa nothing beats the homemade version, especially using my mom's recipe below and you'll be glad you did.

- 1 stick butter cut up in pieces (or 1/3 cup oil)
- 4-5 green Cardamoms slightly pounded using a pestle and mortar
- 1/4 cup slivered almonds
- 1 cup *sooji* or cream of wheat (sooji is available at Indian/ Pakistani markets)
- 2 cups water
- A few drops of lemon yellow food coloring (optional)

- 1 cup sugar
- A pinch of saffron (soaked in 2 tablespoons of water for ½ an hour)
- ¼ cup chopped pistachios for garnish

Heat butter (or oil) in a deep pan. As the butter heats up and starts to melt add the green cardamoms, sauté them for a few seconds (15-20) until they start to lend aroma. Add the slivered almonds and sauté for 20-25 seconds. Stir often for even browning of almonds and adjust the heat to make sure the butter does not change color or burn.

187

Add the sooji (cream of wheat) as you continue to stir. Sauté the sooji, stirring constantly. (This step to sauté sooji is a crucial step; a well sautéed sooji will result in a more delicious halwa. Spend a couple of minutes longer if needed and stir often for even cooking) When sooji begins to have a fried appearance, after about 4-6 minutes add the measured water and the food coloring. Fried sooji starts to absorb the water quickly so lower the flame and stir to blend for even cooking. It will have a thick soup like appearance at this point.

After it boils and bubbles for a couple of minutes, add sugar. Continue to simmer and stir on a very low flame. Add the saffron water and blend it in. Cook another 3-4 minutes. Halwa is done when the melted butter or oil begins to surface around the edges of the pan. Garnish with chopped pistachios. Serve by it self or with parathas or Indian pooris.

Serves: 8-10

Check with Indian/Pakistani cafes in your area, as a lot of them are now serving the traditional 'poori/ channa' breakfast including halwa on Sundays even here in the U.S.

Gulaab Jamun

The recipe I share here evolved over yeas. I worked on it for a long period. I had developed a pretty good variation over time, but felt something was still

missing. Until, during one of my visits to Lahore I stopped at one of Lahore's famous mithaee (sweet) shops to pick up some sweets, and just randomly asked the owner if he would be kind enough to share his gulaab jamun recipe with me. The next thing I knew I was in their kitchen, where he not only gave me a tour of the facility, but introduced me to his halwai (dessert chef) who explained to me the ingredients and techniques. I found my missing link to the puzzle, cream of wheat! This finding alone is worth its weight in gold.

- 1 cup powdered milk
- 1 ¼ cup buttermilk pancake mix
- ¾ cup ricotta cheese
- 2 tablespoons cream of wheat (or sooji, available at Indian/Pakistani markets)
- 2 tablespoons butter or ghee
- 1 egg
- 2-4 tablespoons chopped pistachios for garnish

Mix all of the above listed ingredients in a mixing bowl to form dough. Knead the dough well. If the dough is too sticky add a little more pancake mix to the dough. Form tiny dough balls, about 1"-1½" in diameter and fry in batches in oil heated to 350°. Quickly turn sides with a fork for even browning on all sides. Drain on a paper towel for 5-7 minutes before adding to the hot syrup.

NOTE: If the oil is too hot, the dough balls will brown before cooking through on the inside, and if the oil is not hot enough they will start to crack. Adjust the heat as needed.

NOTE: It is essential that gulaab jamuns are added to the syrup while the syrup and the fried gulaab jamun dough balls are still warm. Gulaab jamuns need to soak up some syrup, and both items need to be fairly warm for that to happen.

Sugar Syrup:
- 3 ½ cups sugar
- 4 cups water
- ¼ teaspoon cardamom
- a pinch of saffron (optional)

Bring all of the above to a boil and boil for 25-30 minutes. Turn off flame and let the syrup cool for about 7-10 minutes. Add all of the fried gulaab jamuns into the syrup.

Serve warm, chilled or at room temperature.
Garnish with chopped pistachios.

Makes about 25 gulaab jamuns

Zarda

(Sweet rice cooked in aromatic light spices and nuts)

Zarda is a traditional dessert served at weddings, during festivals or other special occasions. It is cooked in a syrup base of orange juice and milk or cream, with nuts folded in and flavored with saffron. This may be an acquired taste for some, so I figured if it's not given an opportunity for a taste test-and a courage to present . . . . when will we ever find out how it's going to be received. I have faith in the American palate.

I simply love it, and couldn't resist to share

Zarda with fresh fruit and Crème fraiche

- 1 cup sugar
- 1 cup orange juice (or a mix of orange and tangerine juice)
- 1 cup milk or half and half
- 1 cup rice (*basmati* rice please . . .)
- 6-8 cups of water to boil rice
- 2 tablespoons fresh orange peel (orange part only)
- 4-6 black cloves
- 4-6 green cardamoms
- A few drops of yellow food coloring

- 1/2 stick plus 1 tablespoon butter
- A generous pinch of saffron soaked in 4 tablespoons of warm milk
- ¼ cup shelled pistachios
- ¼ cup almonds

To Serve:
- 1 container of crème fraiche or
- Sarsheer (available at Persian markets)

191

For the Syrup:

Boil the orange juice and sugar for about 10 minutes and then add the milk and boil syrup for another 7-10 minutes. Set aside.

To par boil the rice:

Boil water in a deep pot with a couple of black cloves, two green cardamoms and a tablespoon of orange rind. As soon as the water comes to a boil, add the rice. Watch the rice very closely, as you are only partially boiling the rice; test a few grains after about 7-9 minutes of boiling between your thumb and the forefinger to check for doneness. The rice should be firm in the middle and slightly breakable at the edges. Add the food color and 1 tablespoons of butter, drain rice in a colander.

To complete:

Pre-heat oven to 300°

Heat1/2 stick butter in a medium sauce pan. When the butter is melted and most of the foam has dissolved add 4 cardamoms, 4 black cloves and sauté for a few seconds. Add the almonds and cook the hot butter mixture for a few seconds. Gently add the parboiled rice and fold into the butter mixture. Pour in about 1 cup of the syrup (save the remaining syrup for serving later) and gently mix the rice and syrup together. Add the remaining rind of orange to the pot. Cover and cook on the stove for about five minutes on a low medium flame. Finish cooking in a preheated oven for about 25-35 minutes. Remove from oven and gently fold in the shelled pistachios.

Serve with crème fraiche or 'sarsheer' (available at most Persian stores), and a tablespoon or two of the orange syrup. Garnish with orange rind and mint. Enjoy.

Serves: 8-10

Pistachio Burfee

There is a tradition we have in India and Pakistan to distribute sweets among friends and family when sharing joyous news, for example for a wedding announcement, the birth of a child or any special achievement by a family member like a job promotion or graduation. All of these announcements call for delivering some sweets with the news. So all over India and Pakistan you will see sweet or *'mithaee'* shops with a large variety of colorful sweets tempting the eyes and the sweet tooth. Burfee is a popular variety of sweets, and a vital part of the sweet box or basket.

Pistachio Burfee

Cool before cutting in squares

Cooking Burfee

- 1 stick butter
- ¼ teaspoon ground cardamom pods (from the green cardamom)
- 2 cups ricotta cheese (part skim is o.k.)
- 2 cups powdered milk
- ¼ teaspoon saffron threads (soaked in ½ cup of warm half and half for 20 minutes)
- 1 cup shelled pistachios, finely ground
- ½ cup ground almonds (skinless)
- 1 cup (8 oz.) sugar
- A few drops of green

- food coloring
- A drop or two of lemon
- yellow food coloring

Slice butter into 6 to 8 slices and heat in a sauce pan. Add cardamom powder and cook as you stir for about 1/2 a minute. Add the ricotta cheese, powdered milk and half and half with saffron. Cook stirring over medium to low heat for about 6-10 minutes to allow for excess moisture from the mix to evaporate. At this point add the ground nuts and continue cooking as you keep stirring. As the liquid and excess moisture in the pan begins to evaporate in about 4-6 minutes, the butter will begin to surface around the edges, which is an indication of doneness.

Continue to sauté the mix for another couple of minutes, add sugar and the food color and continue to cook as you stir for another 6-8 minutes. Let the mixture thicken a little as the water from the sugar evaporates. Spread on a 6 x 9 cookie sheet or a pan and let cool for a few hours or overnight. Cut into squares, makes about 32 squares.

Garnish with chopped pistachios

Yields 32 pieces

Kulfi

This traditional Indian/Pakistani version of ice cream is quick to make, rich with nuts and flavored with saffron and cardamom. It is a lovely ending to a summer meal. I start making the kulfi in an ice cream maker, and then freeze it in molds; this keeps the kulfi smooth and creamy. For the individual molds, the 5 oz plastic containers with lids (available at most restaurant supply stores) are a great container to freeze it in, which unmolds with ease for individual servings.

For the Kulfi

- 1 cup Ricotta cheese
- One 12 oz can of evaporated milk
- 1 pint heavy whipping cream
- One 14 oz can condensed sweetened milk
- ½ cup ground almonds
- ½ cup green pistachios
- a pinch of saffron, soaked for 10 minutes in 2 tablespoons of warm cream or milk.
- ½ teaspoon cardamom seeds, ground

Berry topping for the family size mold
- 1 cup sliced strawberries
- 1 cup blueberries
- 1 cup raspberries
- 1 tablespoon sugar

Directions:

Bring the ricotta cheese and the cream to a soft boil, lower heat and let simmer for a few minutes, (2-4 minutes) while stirring constantly until well blended. Cool completely.

In a blender pour in the cooled ricotta and cream mixture, now add all of the other remaining ingredients, and puree everything together until well blended. Make sure the nuts are well pureed with the other ingredients. Pour the contents into an electric ice cream maker and freeze according to the instructions provided for your machine.

Freezing the kulfi mix in an ice cream maker first will keep the frozen kulfi from crystallizing and the final yield will be smooth and creamy.

Spoon the mix from the ice cream maker into individual molds and freeze overnight or for at least 12 hours. For a larger group, transfer the frozen mix from the ice cream maker into your favorite mold and store in the freezer for at least an overnight or until ready to serve.

Un-mold and serve with berries of your choice.

Makes 12 individual molds or one large mold

FIRNI

Serves 8-10

The traditional style of serving firni is in individual sized servings using earthenware pots called a *'thu-thee'* with the top dressed in the finest layer of a real silver film called 'varaq', as seen in the image below. And for your home parties any dessert serving bowl will work. You can garnish it with chopped pistachios and berries of your choice, in place of varaq.

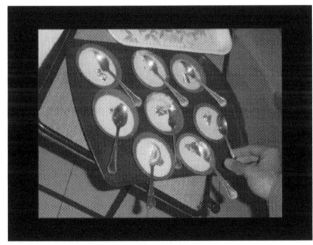

Firni seen served here in 'thu-thees' (clay pots) traditional style.

- 1 carton half and half-1 qt
- 1/2 gallon milk
- 1/2 cup cream of rice or finely ground rice
- 4 small green cardamoms
- 1 cup ground almonds
- 1/4 cup ground pistachios
- 1/4 cup coarsely chopped pistachios
- 4 cups sugar
- 1/2 teaspoon saffron threads soaked for
- 15-30 minutes in ½ cup milk

Boil the half and half and milk with the ground rice, cardamom and ground almonds and pistachios. Save the coarsely chopped pistachios for later use. Keep stirring occasionally on medium to low heat, cook for about an hour to an hour and a half until the pot liquid is reduced to about 1/3 of the original amount.

At this stage keep a very close eye to make sure the contents do not stick to the bottom of the pan and burn. Left unattended it will have a tendency to do that. Stir the pot often and almost constantly. Slow cook on a low flame.

When the mixture has thickened enough to coat the back of the spoon add the sugar and saffron.

Simmer for another 5 to 7 minutes and turn the flame off. Pour into serving dishes and chill completely.

Since waraq are not readily available in the U.S. I garnish firni with chopped pistachios and mint leaves. You can also top with a mix of fresh berries.

Sevion Ka Zarda (Apa's Recipe)

(Steamed Vermicelli with Sautéed Cardamom Topping)

My mother (Apa) was a gifted artist, both, on the canvas and in the kitchen. And here by far, is one of her true masterpieces . . . The beauty of this work of art is that in a few carefully implemented simple steps you can recreate this work of genius, and proudly sign your name on it.

- 4 cups water
- 2 ½ cups sugar
- A nice pinch of saffron
- ½ teaspoon of seeds from green cardamom, coarsely ground
- 2 packages Sevian (Ahmed's Vermicelli from Pakistan*)

* Vermicelli is available at Indian/Pakistani spice stores

For the Tarka or topping (Sautéed cardamom topping)
- ¼ cup of oil
- 1 tablespoon butter for flavoring
- ½ teaspoon more of cardamom seeds

- 4 tablespoons chopped pistachios for garnish

Pre-heat the oven to 250°.

Boil water with sugar, saffron, and the coarsely cracked ½ teaspoon of cardamom seeds. Let boil 3-5 minutes, add vermicelli to the boiling syrup; cook uncovered for 5 minutes, fold the vermicelli into the boiling syrup to coat and soak all sides in the boiling syrup. Cover, reduce heat and let steam for about 5-6 minutes.

Meanwhile in a deep frying pan heat oil and butter together. Add the remaining cardamom seeds in the hot oil and sauté for a few seconds until they begin to sizzle and start to lend their flavor; stir as you sauté, 1-2 minutes. Pour the sautéed cardamom mix; over the vermicelli in the pan.

Cover pan and set in a pre-heated oven for12-15 minutes. Use the middle rack of oven. Garnish with chopped pistachios and serve.

Serves 8-10

Shahee Tukray

There are quite a few variations to the recipe for *shahee tukray* in the Indian/ Pakistani cuisine. This one is from a good friend of mine Rukhsana Abid who is one of the gifted cooks I know. I like this recipe, for many reasons, one of them being that it's a 'quick to fix' variation of the traditional recipe, especially when you are planning to fix *shahee tukray* for a crowd. Your ingredients after being prepped are baked and served out of the same baking dish.

- 1 sliced butter milk bread, edges removed
- Oil for Frying
- 32 oz Ricotta Cheese
- 2 cups ground almonds
- ½ cup slivered almonds
- ½ cup coarsely chopped pistachios
- 4 cups sugar syrup at room temperature (recipe follows)*

*For the sugar syrup:
- 6 cups sugar
- 7 cups water
- A pinch of saffron threads

In a deep sauce pan add the sugar, water and the saffron threads and set the pan over a medium flame. Bring the contents to boil and let the mixture boil for 30-35 minutes. Turn the flame off and let it cool for at least a couple of hours until the syrup comes down to room temperature before using.

Fry the bread slices on both sides until light gold and crisp. Finely grind almonds and mix in the ricotta cheese. Layer the fried toast in an 11X17 glass baking dish, spread half of the almond and ricotta cheese mixture over the bread slices in an even layer, top with half of the slivered almonds and the chopped pistachios.

Put a second layer of fried toast and top with the remaining almond and ricotta cheese mix. Sprinkle the remaining slivered almonds and the chopped pistachios on top of the cheese spread. Pour the prepared sugar syrup on top. Pre heat oven to 325°, bake the bread mixture for 25-30 minutes. Cool, and serve.

Serves 10-12

Almond Squares

This dessert recipe is another one of Rukhsana's wonderful recipes. It is quick to make and simply delicious.

Ingredients:
- 6 eggs
- 1 Stick of Butter
- 1 Cup Sugar
- 1 Cup Powdered Milk
- 1 cup peeled almonds finely ground (lightly toasted if desired, then ground)
- A pinch of Saffron threads

DIRECTIONS:

Mix all of the above ingredients in a blender or a food processor. Spread contents in a 9"x11" baking dish and bake for 30 minutes at 325 degrees oven. Cool completely before cutting into squares or diamonds, and serve

Serves 10-12

Chilled Mango Soufflé

Ask anyone from Pakistan or India which fruit they consider the 'king of all fruits', chances are they will say, 'mango'. It is the Almighty's sweet reward to the people of sub-continent for enduring the long humid summer, as it's a very seasonal summer fruit of that region. Mango is such a celebrated treat in that part of the world that even the most fanatic calorie counters opt to put themselves on 'mango diet' rather than miss out on the season altogether. The following recipe is sure to give a classic ending to any meal.

For step one:
- ¼ cup strained fresh lemon juice
- 2 ½ cups pureed mango
  (Preferably pureed canned mango imported from India and available at most Indian grocery stores)
- 2 envelopes unflavored gelatin

For step 2:
- 1½ cup sugar
- 9 egg yolks
- 2 teaspoon corn starch
- 1 ½ cup half and half heated in a saucepan
- 1 tablespoon grated rind of lemon

For step#3:
- 7 egg whites
- A pinch of salt
- ¼ tea spoon cream of tartar
- 4 tablespoon sugar

For step #4:
- 1 cup chilled whipping cream
- ½ cup mango puree chilled well
- Well chilled mixing bowl and beaters

Directions:

Step #1:

To soften gelatin combine the lemon juice and the pureed mango in a shallow dish or a bowl and sprinkle the gelatin on top.

Step #2:

Using an electric beater or a wire whip beat the sugar into the yolks in a mixing bowl until the mixture is pale and lemon colored, about two minutes. Beat in the cornstarch.

Then, in a thin stream, beat in the hot half and half. Pour the egg yolk mixture into a saucepan, add the lemon peel and cook over moderate heat stirring constantly with a wooden spoon until the mixture thickens enough to coat the spoon lightly; and heated to 170 °. Do not let the mixture boil or the yolks may curdle. But heat enough to thicken the custard properly. Remove from heat and immediately beat in the Mango/ lemon mixture with gelatin.

Step #3:

In a clean dry bowl, beat the egg whites until foamy, and then add the salt and the cream of tartar and continue beating until soft peaks are formed, now add the sugar and continue beating until stiff peaks are formed. Fold the beaten egg whites into the custard and chill, folding occasionally to keep the mixture from separating.

Step # 4:

When the custard has cooled off well (but not set) proceed to step #4. Start to beat the chilled whipping cream in the chilled bowl using the chilled beaters until it has doubled in volume. (If the weather is hot chill the whipping cream carton, the mixing bowl and the beaters in the freezer for about 30 minutes to an hour before starting to beat the cream) Fold the cream and the mango puree into the cold mango custard. If the custard has started to set you can smooth it out using electric beaters.

To serve as a chilled soufflé surround soufflé dish with a waxed paper collar to stand 3" above the dish. Pour in the mango custard mixture and chill until set.

Peel off paper just before serving and if necessary smooth the outside edge of the soufflé with a knife dipped in warm water.

You can chill it in your favorite mold and then un-mold it before serving by dipping the mold in hot water and quickly running a knife around the inside edge of the mold. To un-mold, cover the mold with the serving dish and turn the mold upside down.

Garnish with your choice of berries.

Serves 8-10

Hot and Cold Beverages

A small collection of some summer thirst quenchers
and 'cool me downers' and some help you 'cozy up'
hot drinks for cold winter nights. The collection of
drinks in the Indian/Pakistani cuisine offers great
options for all seasons. I am including a small sampling
of recipes of drinks favored during summer time
and a some enjoyed during winter.

Doodhi

A delicious milk drink packed with nuts and flavored with ground cardamom and saffron.

This family recipe runs back for generations in our 'kashmiri' family, and was enjoyed without fail several times every winter. It is specifically a winter drink perfect for chilly nights.

Ingredients:
- 1 gallon milk
- ½ cup ground peeled almonds
- ½ cup ground pistachios
- ½ cup 'char magaz' these are actually melon
- seeds peeled (available at the Indian spice stores)
- Sliced dried coconut (optional)
- 5-8 green cardamom pods cracked and seeds ground
- ½ tea spoon turmeric ground
- ½ stick butter
- ¼ cup vegetable oil
- ½ teaspoon saffron threads soaked in ½ cup warm milk
- Sugar to taste
- Pinch of salt

Directions:

Heat butter and oil in a deep pot and add the cracked green cardamoms with the ground seeds, sauté in the oil and butter for a couple of minutes, until the cardamom seeds start to lend their flavor to the oil. Keep stirring to keep the butter from turning brown. Add the ground turmeric and sauté for another 2-3 minutes.

Add milk, and as it starts to boil add the ground nuts and the melon seeds (char magaz). Set heat level where the milk boils slowly without boiling over. Continue to boil until it is reduced by about $1/3$ its original amount and is slightly thickened.

Add the soaked saffron and simmer for another half hour. Add sugar and serve hot with extra ground nuts on the side.

Yield: 18-20 small cups

Mango Lassi

Lassi is a popular thirst quencher especially during the humid summer months in India and Pakistan. Mango is a popular choice for a lassi drink. I usually make this recipe with the canned mango pulp imported from India and available at Indian spice stores. My reason for using this canned mango pulp is simple, as, when it comes to flavor there is no match for Indian and Pakistani mangoes-period.

- 1 6oz carton lemon yogurt
- 6 oz canned mango pulp* or 1 cup fresh mango
- 6 oz water or 6 oz milk
- 1 cup ice
- 2 tablespoons sugar
- 2 tablespoons lemon juice

Pour all ingredients in a blender and blend for a few seconds. Serve with additional ice or as is.

* Available at Indian spice stores.

Almond Lassi

Make this lassi for individual servings or for your party punch bowl to serve at your next gathering, and it will be received with much zest and passion, especially for those summer bashes. It is fun, refreshing and delicious. There is not too much of an exact science to the proportions here; all you need to do is to make sure you are including all the ingredients listed below in your preferred variation, I go for a richer consistency so I tend not to dilute too much with water. There are no rights or wrongs here just different variations. So take charge and feel free to play with this recipe.

- 1 6 oz carton lemon yogurt
- 6 oz cold water or 6 oz milk
- ¼ cup finely chopped almonds
- A few drops of almond flavoring (optional)
- 1 cup ice
- 2 tablespoons sugar
- 2 tablespoons lemon juice

Pour all of the above ingredients in a blender and blend for a few seconds. Serve with additional ice or as is.

Garnish with fresh mint leaves and lemon wedges

Note: If making for a party punch bowl, serve with a lot of ice.

Doodh Chai

(Tea brewed with milk)

Please bear with me for a sec here . . . as I am about to inject some fun. My philosophy is it's only life-let's not start taking it too seriously now. O K enough apologies, so here it is: I am including this recipe here first and foremost for my daughters who love 'pakee chai', (or the truck stop chai, as we call it in Punjab). And secondly, for all of those friends that I love dearly, who fondly assign the chai making duty over in my direction, with the compliment, "Farhana, you make the best chai". I am not sure if sharing my 'secret recipe' here is going to get me off the hook completely, but I thought was worth a try.

- 6 cups water
- 2 ½ cups milk
- ½ teaspoon ground green cardamom
- 1" piece of stick cinnamon
- 3-5 black cloves
- 5-6 bags of black tea

Directions:

Boil water in a deep pan; add the green cardamoms, the stick of cinnamon and the cloves. Once the water comes to a boil, add the tea bags and turn heat down to simmer, cover the pot and let the tea brew for 1 minute in the simmering water. Turn off the flame, keeping the pot covered let the tea brew for another 3 to 5 minutes.

In the meantime start to boil the milk in a separate pan; you can also microwave the milk. Add the hot milk to the brewed tea. Turn the heat on at the lowest setting, partially uncover the pot and let slow boil and simmer for 3 minutes. Pour in a pre-warmed tea pot and serve.

Note: During the cold winter months I will usually warm my serving cups with hot water before pouring the tea in the cups. And always pre heat your tea pot, to make sure the tea holds its temperature until served.

Yield: 4-6 cups

Shared steps and procedures for a range of recipes

You will find most of the guidelines and steps listed below under some individual recipes as well and may seem in excess here.
I decided still to collect
them all and list them in one place for ease of quick reference.

Garam Massala Recipe

Ingredients:
- 2 tablespoons black pepper corns
- 1 tablespoon cloves
- 1, 1/2" piece of stick cinnamon
- 2 black cardamoms
- 6 tablespoons cumin seeds

Directions:
Grind all of the above spices together in an electric grinder for a few seconds until finely ground. Store the fresh ground garam massala in an airtight container.

Toasting cumin seeds:
Heat a non stick small frying pan and add a teaspoon of cumin seeds to the heated pan. Stir with a wooden spoon for a few seconds, about 15-20 seconds and remove from heat. Continue stirring for even toasting until lightly toasted but not burnt. Transfer the toasted seeds into a bowl or a plate to stop the cooking process. Toasted seeds can be lightly ground using a mortar and pestle, grinding the toasted seeds brings out more of their flavor.

Homemade cheese:

- 1 gallon whole milk
- 3/4 cup lemon juice (fresh squeezed or bottled)

Heat milk in a deep cooking pot. As the milk starts to boil add the lemon juice and stir. Continue to boil for 3-4 minutes; the acid will separate the milk, the

215

solid curd will rise to the top separating from the whey below. Reduce heat and let the liquid simmer for 2-3 minutes, turn heat off and allow the pot to cool for 10-15 minutes.

Strain the whey in a strainer lined with a double layer of cheese cloth. Twist and tie the cheese cloth tightly, let the cheese drain completely, about 3 to 4 hours.

Untie and wrap the formed cheese in plastic, refrigerate until ready to use (can be refrigerated for approx. 2 to 3 days). Cut in cubes, fry lightly to a soft golden color, drain on paper towels, and season warm cubes with salt. Fried cheese pieces can be frozen in a zip lock bag.

A Shortcut Tip:

You can make cheese at home using the recipe above if you so desire. Knowing that ready made Indian cheese (*paneer*) is now widely available at Indian spice stores, and is a great alternative I would encourage its use in recipes calling for Indian cheese in this book. Since I am a fan of short cuts and work reduction in the kitchen, I like to employ any trim down technique I can get my hands on.

Frying paneer (Cheese):
When frying cheese use the following steps and precautions.

Indian cheese, homemade or store bought tends to hold moisture and when moist cheese is added to the hot oil, the oil may start to splatter. To avoid the oil from splashing, let the sliced cheese sit at room temperature in a plate for about 15-20 minutes. Preferably, spread the cheese pieces out in a single layer, this will allow for most of the moisture to evaporate and keep the oil splatter at minimal.

Chopping Cilantro:

We use this herb a lot in Indian/Pakistani cooking as you will see it in my recipes. One word of caution I would add is about chopping cilantro, and a couple of things to keep in mind for optimum flavor from this herb:

i)   Chop the stems and leaves together, do not discard the stems.

ii) Make sure not to over chop cilantro or you will loose all the flavor of the herb; over chopping somehow alters its natural aroma.

Making Chicken Stock:

Chicken stock for the Indian/Pakistani recipes is one 'cooking aid' I would <u>insist</u> you make at home. You will be so much happier with its flavor and on how that flavor will elevate the quality and taste of the dish you are fixing. If you however are using the store bought stock, boil it for a few minutes with the spices and herbs listed below before using.

Ingredients:
- 2 chicken legs or thighs
- 2 cloves of garlic
- 1 teaspoon salt
- ¼ teaspoon black pepper corns
- 6-8 black cloves
- 1 black cardamom
- ½ a stick of cinnamon
- 4 cups water

Directions:

Put the ingredients listed above in a deep pot, cook over medium high heat. Boil for 20-25 minutes, reduce flame, cover the pot and simmer for another 20 minutes. Strain into a container and reserve for use. Prepared chicken stock can be frozen in a container with a tight lid for later use.

To purée ginger and garlic:

Having a batch of pureed ginger and garlic stored in the refrigerator in an airtight plastic container or a jar with a tight lid is a great timesaver. It is easy to make, just a few seconds in the food processor is all it needs. Peeled garlic is available at most markets and grocery stores.

I usually use 1 cup of peeled garlic cloves and about a 4" piece of fresh ginger, wash the ginger well you can remove the skin or leave it on, but remove the knotty parts or dried up edges with a knife. Put both items in the processor and process until finely pureed.

About Chef Farhana

Farhana Sahibzada is originally from Lahore, Pakistan. She is the former chef and owner of cinnamon STIX, a café and catering business she established and operated in Woodland Hills, California.

Farhana has been teaching Indian/Pakistani cooking for over 20 years in southern California. In addition to teaching classes at her café she has taught cooking classes for Pierce College, Let's get cookin' in Westlake Village, California, Gelson's super Markets, Williams-Sonoma, Whole Foods Markets, The culinary art's college at the Art's Institute in Santa Monica California (where she is a regular visiting guest chef and instructor), Southern California's Culinary Institute in South Pasadena, California and many other local cooking schools and gourmet food markets.

Her classes focus on simplifying the art of Indian cooking and offer simple and quick versions for classic and popular recipes of the Indian/Pakistani cuisine.

In addition to cooking her native cuisine, Farhana's interest and passion of cooking also includes gourmet American and European desserts and pastries.

Being a teacher at heart and eager to share her learning, she takes the extra mile in her description and elaboration of the step by steps of Indian/Pakistani cooking and recipes within this book. She does that with the desire to help the users of the book succeed without fuss and frustration. Don't be surprised if you find this book to be a different read than your typical cookbook. Actually expect it to be *atypical* as it has been carefully crafted to be just that.

In addition to cooking, Farhana's hobbies and interests include drawing, water color, airbrush, gardening and long walks. Farhana lives in southern California with her husband. She is the mother of two daughters Mehnaz and Naureen.

To see full color pictures of recipes in this book go to Farhana's blog: www. farhanacooks.blogspot.com
Email: farhana22430@hotmail.com
Website: www.flavorfulshortcuts.com

UNDER THE STARS IN SAUDI ARABIA

Jeddah, Mecca, Taif. In every city, the desert
smelled of violets. Weekends, we ate french fries

on the beach, watched veiled women charge
into the Red Sea. My sister and I built sand castles

with golden domes, called each other "booger"
and "butt head" over plastic toy telephones. Our

parents always drove to the coast at night when
the stars blinked Arabic, the dunes shadowed

and desolate. I often gazed up at the sky, stories
of flying carpets and silver wands behind my eyes.

I was seven—knew no poems, no poets then, except
the spoken verses of the Quran, which were sung

at the Kaba in voices rich as henna. Claimed
with tongues that kissed each word. Something

in me stirred amid those high mosque walls. I'd
listen to the call for prayer with my head tilted up

as though the sounds funneled out some cloud:
ethereal, loud. I'd listen with eyes closed, my head

draped in a purple scarf, thinking neither about hair
nor covering yet, but the arresting tide of words

rising, falling—calling in a language I didn't
understand but felt like a hand brushing the ear.

Just hearing the holy suras made me feel wiser,
older. Those weekends we drifted between towns,

I never worried about disloyalty. The three years
we lived in Saudi, I never inked a line of simile. Yet

on Saturday nights, I mouthed Arabic recitations
with my lips—carried Mecca in the grip of my memory.

Under the stars, I wrote in the sand with my feet,
ate kababs salted with splashes of the Red Sea.
                    Mehnaz Sahibzada

Tongue-tied:
A Memoir in Poems

Mehnaz Sahibzada

Tongue-Tied:

Is a collection of poems by Mehnaz Sahibzada.
Mehnaz is a Pakistani/American,
writer and poet born in Lahore, Pakistan
and raised in Southern California.
Mehnaz is a well known figure in the literary and poetry circles
in the Los Angeles area.
Her story, "The Alphabet Workbook", was published
in Ellery Queen Mystery Magazine
Her poems have appeared in publications such as Asia Writes,
Mascara Literary Review
The Journal of Pakistan studies, Cahoots Magazine, The Pedestal Magazine, and
An Anthology of California Poets
To learn more about Mehnaz, visit her at:
www.mehnazsahibzada.blogspot.com

Tongue Tied is a collection of poetry stemming form
Mehnaz's rich heritage and background

The book is published by Finishing Line Press

223

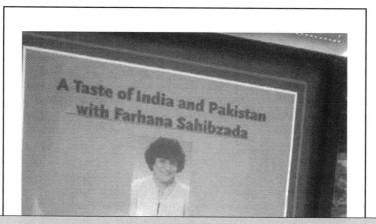

An announcement poster for one of Farhana's recent cooking classes held at Whole Foods, a natural foods market.

Student feedback and comments

"Good Work" . . . . JC, Woodland Hills

"We had a great time in a fun and relaxed atmosphere . . . .
terrific experience" . . . . LM, Thousand Oaks

"Very informative" . . . . BM. Tarzana

"Fabulous! Would highly recommend!" . . . . Nancy, Canoga Park

"FANTASTIC! Great class!!" . . . . Janet, Woodland Hills

"Loved the instructor, she was knowledgeable and made me feel
relaxed!" . . . Judy, WH

Let's Give Credit Where Credit is due!

Index

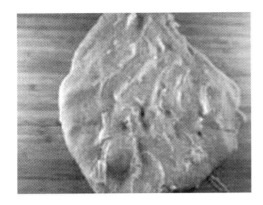

227

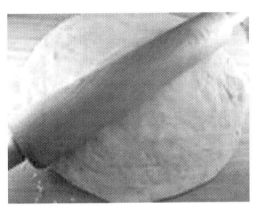